PROOF OF THE AFTERLIFE

The Dead don't die. True Tales of the Afterlife

STEPH YOUNG

Copyright © 2022 by *Steph Young*

All rights reserved. No part of this book may be used or reproduced by any means, graphic, electronic, or mechanical, including photocopying, recording, taping, or by any information storage retrieval system, without the written permission of the publisher except in the case of brief quotations embodied in critical articles and reviews.

CONTENTS

Excerpts 1

Introduction 2

Chapter One: 'I could clearly see white, bony, long tapered fingers and a bony arm'. 6

Chapter Two: 'The spirit's face was right in front of me, so close to me. He was beaming with joy, smiling, and laughing.' 13

Chapter Three: 'I was being prodded and poked and tickled – by invisible hands.' 29

Chapter Four: 'The spirit girl weighed 77 lbs.' 39

Chapter Five: 'The spirit man took a seat on the music stool and proceeded to play half a dozen perfectly harmonious chords, using both hands.' 53

Chapter Six: "The eyes, and my God, the eyelids are moving!" 65

Chapter Seven: 'Perhaps the most staggering incident was when a spirit materialized in the room.' 105

Chapter Eight: "How would you like to feel the hand of a man who's been dead for one hundred years?" 112

Chapter Nine: "There he stood. Hair - spiky as always. Eyes - so, so blue." 137

Chapter Ten: "I had the pleasure of seeing a manifestation of Mr W.T. Stead. His body from the waist up, was quite distinct." 144

Chapter Eleven: "We had a full height, full materialization of a person that was fully recognized by the details of their dress and their mannerisms." 152

Chapter Twelve: 'One Christmas Eve, a stranger suddenly appeared before him, though the door was closed.' 172

Chapter Thirteen: 'Father Gemelli was astonished to hear the voice of his dead father saying, "Of course I shall help you. I'm always with you." 194

Chapter Fourteen: 'The materialised people came out of the cabinet sometimes two or three at a time.... After a while, you forgot you were conversing with so-called dead people.' 198

Chapter Fifteen: 'The realisation dawned on him it had not been the medium he had greased but what it purported to be... a fully materialised spirit form.... The man looked up at me, his eyes wide, terrified.' 206

Chapter Sixteen: 'Her weight seemed scarcely as much as that of a child of eight years, but her arm felt solid upon my shoulder, and the lips that caressed me were as natural as life.' 223

Chapter Seventeen: 'Mrs. Houseman said in a matter of fact voice, that she had been cured of a crippling affliction by a surgeon who had returned from the dead to operate on her.' 235

Chapter Eighteen: 'Lilley had an unusual use for ectoplasm; sometimes he would use it to grow new living tissue in patients.' 257

Conclusion 269

Glossary.. 270

Excerpts

'My little son spoke to me… and afterwards materialized within 5 inches of my face. My little boy asked for his mummy and spoke about a bottle. "Don't you remember? You put it in my hand when I was in my coffin?"

'Dr. Reynolds appeared, fully materialised. He chatted to me just as any doctor would chat with a patient in his consulting room, taking my head in his materialised hands and examining it.'

'The face was quite solid, without colouring but obviously alive; the lips moved in an attempt to answer me… "I have no pain now; I do not suffer as I used to … isn't it glorious?"

'A number of spirit children materialised. They were mischievous and set-about ruffling-up a gentleman guest's hair, pulling his tie and tickling his legs, with yelps of delight.'

"How would you like to feel the hand of a man who's been dead for one hundred years?"

Introduction

This book is the result of two year's intensive study of physical mediumship, both past and present; of the 'dead' physically returning, of 'spirit doctors' curing "incurable" patients, of interviewing numerous mediums, and of joining a development circle in order to become a medium myself. To say it's been a wild ride would be an understatement. I've stepped into a mysterious, compelling, addictive and utterly mind-blowing arena, where I've seen things I never thought possible; where I've communicated directly with family in the afterlife, had spirits take over my body, and felt the physical touch of spirits. I've heard and seen 'dead' people, been operated on by a "spirit doctor", and I've been poked, prodded and tickled by spirit children. Of course, unless it's personally seen, felt, and experienced, this is all understandably very hard to believe, and I'm as sceptical as the next person; perhaps even more so. I'd encourage the reader to venture into their own exploration to discover this proof, that no matter how much it defies our logical, rational mind, these things can and really do happen, as I've discovered for myself; that the dead don't really die: they're still around us, all the time.

Physical mediumship may be going on across the land in small closed home circles, but they usually remain private and do not get known about these days, while in years gone-by, thousands of people would get to experience these things. With the invention of television and its multitude of channels to watch, with the internet, gaming, mobile phones; everyone is spoiled for choice when it comes to evening entertainment. In the old days, there were no televisions, no mobile phones, no internet, and often very little money too. Spiritualism was readily and enthusiastically experimented with in the comfort of people's own homes, often for such entertainment purposes, but also because after the two World Wars, there were so many families in mourning and desperate to be reunited with their dead sons and husbands, fathers and grandfathers. Just like a family might have gathered together and played a game of cards or parlour games; many families were creating Ouija boards or attempting table-tipping, or simply sitting in the dark and waiting in hope, endeavouring to receive some kind of communication from their dead; or they would hear about a séance from neighbours or friends, and many would go to a local Spiritualist Church. These days, Spiritualist Churches still exist, though they're far from packed nowadays, and it's harder to find a local development circle, for most of them simply don't exist anymore, or don't advertise for members and are known only by word of mouth. It's certainly no longer a past-time of families across the land anymore. At the turn of the 20th Century, the medium John Campbell Sloan would hold open seances at his house in Scotland, where he would demonstrate direct voice phenomena; where voices would be heard in the room, but they were not coming from Sloan himself. The medium Alec Harris would produce spirit materialisations – where "dead" people literally walked around the seance room and shook hands with the guests and held conversations with them. Investigators like Edward Brackett and Colonel Henry Steel Olcott would weigh materialised spirits on weighing scales, and surgeons who had died would come back to operate on patients through the hands of mediums like Isa Northage, Jessie Thomas, Tom Pilgrim, or William Lilley who carried out 'spirit operations' in front of crowds of witnesses, who would testify before a court to the truth of what they had seen; and there would be x-rays and hospital records to prove it. The medium Harry Edwards would hold public demonstrations, to a packed Royal Albert Hall in London with thousands watching him carry out a live healing or give highly accurate evidential messages. Steven Upton, former tutor at the Arthur Findlay College of Spiritualism and psychic sciences tells me that when Edwards was alive, he received literally millions of letters from around the world, asking for healing from the spirits; such was his success rate. Modern demonstrations of mediumship very rarely include physical mediumship or healings now; yet Edwards would receive a 'veritable Niagara of testimony,' from people who had been healed by the spirits who worked through him. Yes, there were charlatans too, as there are in every profession and every walk of life; but medical records and x-rays showing tumours have disappeared cannot be argued with. Today, I've found some more mediums who can still perform these "miracles."

The purpose of this book is to shine a light on some of these compelling accounts, of spirits healing "incurable" people, of the "dead" physically returning to speak with and embrace their loved ones, and to show you just how close to us the spirit world really is; if only you would dare to discover….

CHAPTER ONE

'I could clearly see white, bony, long tapered fingers and a bony arm'.

As I drove through the densely tree-lined country lanes in the heart of the Surrey countryside, and pulled up at a remote house, nestled among a forest of the tallest trees, I wondered what I had got myself into. I hadn't told anyone where I was going. No-one would know where I was if I didn't come back. I sat pondering this in my car as the front door opened and the loveliest lady came towards me, greeting me and welcoming me inside. Too late to back out now, I thought. I'd come for "psychic surgery." I was seriously ill and I'd come for spirits to operate on me – like real doctors in hospitals. At the same time, I felt utterly ridiculous. That's why I hadn't told anyone where I was going. How could I? How was I supposed to explain that? It sounded too silly for words; and, of course I didn't believe in it. I'd thought to myself, "Well, this will be a good experience for my research; after all, how can you write about such things, if you don't experience them first hand?" But I believed it was a complete waste of time too. I mean, who would believe in any of this, realistically? I began to feel rather irritated with myself, and wished I'd decided to spend my time doing something more useful or enjoyable. I was already calculating in my head how long it would take me to drive back home, and which route I'd take. But I'd booked an appointment, and for the sake of a couple of hours, I'd better go through with it now, I reasoned. I just wouldn't tell anyone I had. All these thoughts were running through my head as I stepped through the front door and into the most beautiful old country house, and instantly I felt the most peaceful atmosphere imaginable. Perhaps I was imagining it, but immediately, I felt at ease, and soon we were joined by the husband; the clairvoyant through which the spirits were going to "operate" on me.

The sense of my own ridiculousness persisted, but at least I was meeting the most charming and charismatic couple, who could not have been more welcoming. They'd been clairvoyants and spiritual healers for many decades, and we chatted for quite a while. In fact, the conversation turned to my scepticism of many of the mediums and healers from the past to the present, and their scandalous trickery and outright fraud. Surprisingly, they agreed with me several times and mentioned their own rather disappointing experiences over the years too. Like any profession and in any walk of life, there are some mediums in the past, and still today, who profit by pretending to be able to contact the lost loved ones of grieving people, or trick people at seances into believing a spirit is walking about in the room; but there are many more genuine mediums too, as we will discover in this book. Well, after an hour or so of chatting, sitting in their living room which was full of old books and ancient artefacts, I was asked to hop onto a treatment bed for the healing session to begin.

Lying there in the semi-darkness, with a couple of small lights on, I closed my eyes and the couple got to work. I quite hoped it would be over with quickly. Soft music played in the background and I lay there thinking, "Well, this is not going to do any good at all." I felt stupid, and found myself thinking about the work I needed to do when I got back home, the list increasing as I continued to ruminate. I thought about the rest of my week too, and went through my diary in my mind, for the sake of doing something, rather than simply lying there and doing nothing. I found it very difficult to just relax and lay there. About twenty minutes later, I suddenly felt the sharpest sensations inside my body, as if a scalpel was being used on me! It hurt - not excruciatingly, but it was very uncomfortable and I wanted it to stop, but I was also intrigued. I opened my eyes a fraction - surely, they weren't actually operating on me! I saw both healers standing on either side of me, and I could clearly see their hands. Neither of them were touching that part of my body; they were no-where near it, and they were not holding any scalpels either! What I did see was a hand and an arm - exactly like you might see on an x-ray image. I could clearly see white, bony, long tapered fingers and a bony arm, hovering right over the part of my body where it was hurting. I closed my eyes thinking I had gone entirely mad; that I had to be imagining it, but when I opened my eyes again, I could still see the arm and fingers. I know, or at least, I believe, that there are other "psychic surgeons" out there who are simply charlatans, who probably simply use sleight of hand, or the power of suggestion; but that was not the case here. I couldn't have been more sceptical when I'd walked into their house, and as I'd lain there, feeling entirely ridiculous; and yet I did not imagine this pain and discomfort, and gripping, scrapping sensations inside of me. They were too real. Of course, just about every rational person will dismiss this account, quite understandably, but I know what I saw and I know what I felt, and I can't change that. Make of it what you will, but I can't dismiss it because it felt so physical, and, I'm not in the habit of seeing x-ray arms and hands, and those bony fingers - but that's what I saw, take it or leave it! I've questioned myself regularly since, of course, but what I can't forget are those sharp, gripping, scrapping, cutting sensations inside my body. It wasn't on the surface of my body - it was very deep inside me; and it felt like claws or fingernails, or a scalpel.

Prior to this, I'd been to other spiritual healers before, including visiting the Harry Edwards Healing Sanctuary in Shere. I'd never felt anything, nor seen anything. That isn't to say that no healing took place; it's just that, apparently unlike most other patients, I never could feel anything happening, and this was also why I'd had no expectations before I went to this couple's house in the heart of the countryside. Over time, as I've got to know the couple in the countryside very well and become great friends with them, the husband who carried out my "psychic surgery" told me that it all began for him when he was working as an executive. He would regularly receive phone calls from a lady client, whose manner was particularly brusque and rather rude. After months of putting up with her phone calls, one day he finally snapped and answered her back; to which she replied, "Ah, I see, you're one of us!" He had no idea what she meant, but he found himself being invited to go to a suburban house where a psychic development circle met each week. Before long, he found himself developing the ability to communicate with the dead. One night, not long after he'd joined, he was given the message to go to a community centre in South London, where once a week a healing clinic took place. When he arrived there, the healer in charge told him to simply observe the proceedings, but shortly afterwards, the healer changed his mind and asked why he was just standing there!

Rather swiftly, the husband found himself treating patients too, but with no idea how to do it or what to do, other than to rest his hands on their backs! That same day, the healer suddenly announced he had decided to retire and that he had appointed the husband to take over, with immediate effect!

It was not long after this that the husband began to give healing to a man who had come to the community centre with a bad leg. The man was limping badly and barely mobile. As the husband placed his hands on the man's back, little knowing what else to do, he suddenly heard a voice in his head, talking to him, telling him to cut the man's leg open! He thought he had to be imagining it, or was simply losing his mind, but the voice kept on urging him to do it, telling him, "Pick up the scalpel!" He could see a scalpel now too, clairvoyantly, and he couldn't stop thinking he was going completely mad, but the voice was so persistent; it wouldn't stop demanding that he cut the man open, and so eventually, he found himself grasping the invisible scalpel in his hand and making cutting gestures along the man's leg. "Open him up!" the voice kept saying, and so he did. Not literally cutting the man's leg, but making the gestures with his hand as the voice continued telling him what to do next, so that in the end, he was performing an operation as expertly as a surgeon in a hospital operating theatre, even sewing the man's leg back up with stitches when he was finished, yet all the while thinking he was going insane! Meanwhile, the man sat patiently, showing no signs of distress, no agony, and really being none the wiser about what was going on, and when it was finished, the man calmly got up and left. The following week, the man returned to say that when he'd got back home, his wife had been rather surprised to see him jump over the garden gate rather than hobble through it as he usually did! His leg was completely cured, he declared.

CHAPTER TWO

'The spirit's face was right in front of me, so close to me. He was beaming with joy, smiling, and laughing.'

Dennis Barrett stood on the platform at his local Spiritualist Church. He was giving a demonstration of mediumship, and he pointed to a woman in the audience, telling her that her deceased mother was with him. He began to describe in detail a necklace her mother was wearing, saying, "She tells me she's proud of her beauties." After the demonstration was over, the daughter came up to speak to him, and she told him she was certain it had been her mother because she had a particular habit of standing in front of the mirror adjusting her clothes, "Especially around her bust!" The daughter said she would tell her mother to stop being so vain, and her mother would reply, "What's the matter with you, I'm proud of these beauties." The daughter then explained that these were the exact words she'd heard her mother say so many times. "I could see her there, pulling at her dress so it showed the shape of her boobs!" Dennis had thought her mother had been referring to a necklace – not her bust! Dennis was an ordinary, working-class man. He'd worked on the railways and as a fireman in his hometown of Bristol, England, in the 1950's and '60's. Little could he have known then that soon he would become the most extraordinary physical medium and spiritual healer. Up until then, he'd led a simple, happy life; but when his wife asked him for a divorce, he found himself living in a tiny bedsit with only a one bar heater. The winter was bitterly cold, and he was understandably miserable and very lonely, and he found himself going to Spiritualist Churches in the evenings; but not for the usual reasons. He admits that he went there to stave off the crippling loneliness he felt, and to keep warm! In his home town at the time, there were so many Spiritualist Churches that he could go to a different one each night, so he took to doing the rounds.

At the first Church he went to, he bumped into an old work colleague, who instantly told him that although he might not realise it yet, Dennis was a spiritual healer. Dennis had no idea what the man was going on about; how could he be a healer without knowing it? But more people, at other Spiritualist Churches, began to say the same thing to him too. One night, a woman at Church offered him a lift home – but when he got in the car, she immediately asked him to heal her back. He had no idea what to do, and in fact, he says he wondered if she was propositioning him! He considered getting out of the car, but she was so insistent that eventually he simply placed his hand on her back, not knowing what else to do. Then, within just a few moments, as Jack Angelo relates in Barrett's autobiography, the woman proclaimed that the pain in her back had disappeared. After this, word quickly spread and other people began approaching Dennis, asking him to heal them too. Dennis would place his hands on them, still completely befuddled about why he was doing this and how it could possibly work, but their ailments would disappear. Dennis could not understand how this could be happening, and in an attempt to get some answers he joined a psychic development circle. The circle members were very committed and they sat every week, even at Christmas.

By now, Dennis had met a lady through the churches and they'd got married. She sat in the circle too, along with a lady called Eunice, who was the widow of a blind medium called Ricky. After Ricky had died, she'd continued to receive letters addressed to him from members of the public wishing to use his psychic services. Dennis found that he could 'read' the letters without opening them. He would send replies back, and it quickly became apparent, when the correspondent wrote again, that Dennis' replies had answered their queries or problems precisely. Spirits were telling him the answers, and soon, their voices would speak directly through him too. Males, female, it made no difference. His voice would change into theirs! Interestingly, Dennis explains, 'Contrary to popular belief, we do not contact the spirits – they contact us when we make ourselves available to them and tune in... we certainly do not contact the 'dead' ... we don't need to. They are so eager to tell their loved ones they are still alive and to give them proof of this... It is a sadness to them that there aren't enough mediums to go round.' Although Dennis says we don't contact spirit, they contact us, in the home circle that I sit in, in South West London, we do sometimes request contact from specific spirits, and receive it, although it can't be demanded or ordered. For example, one night we were working in pairs, and we had to take turns to say which dead family member or friend we wanted the partner we were working with to try to communicate with. My partner, a medium who I vaguely knew from the circle but did not know anything about her family or private life, requested that I try to communicate with a deceased friend of hers. All she gave me was his name, no other details. At the time, having only joined the home circle a couple of months before this, and only meeting once a week for a couple of hours, I had no idea who her friends had been or who her family members were, whether alive or dead. None of us really know anything about each other – which is perfect – because the more we know about each other, the more it becomes possible for us to 'cold read' – using what we know about them, and mistaking this as messages from spirit. So, I tried to see if the spirit of my partner's friend would come forward and communicate with me. As soon as I closed my eyes, I could see a young man with curly dark hair standing so close to me. It doesn't always happen like this for me – in fact, at this stage, being a beginner, I very often struggle to get the initial contact. My tutor will say to me, "They're standing right behind you!" or, "Their hand is on your shoulder!" but I often still can't see them or sense them. But this time, the spirit's face was right in front of me, so close to me, and full of such vibrant energy. He was beaming with joy, smiling, and laughing; he appeared to be ecstatic. It took me unaware, and it was the last thing I had been expecting. Often, I struggle to see their facial features, and if I can't sense anyone there, I immediately slip into anxiousness, thinking I'm just going to draw a blank. However, this time, the spirit was impossible not to see – he was so close to my face. My partner asked if I could find out about his death. Instantly, I said, "It wasn't meant to happen." I didn't think about these words – they just popped immediately into my mind and just as quickly out of my mouth, like a compulsion to say it, and my words came out spit-fire fast. Sometimes, I see the words written in big letters. Other times, the words simply jump out of my mouth before I've had any time to consider them.

Proof of the Afterlife

In this case, my partner expressed relief at the words I'd said. She explained that the young man had been her best friend when they were teenagers and he'd died in a way that looked like it could have been suicide. She'd never known if he'd purposely done it, or not. The young man in spirit was showing me, with his beaming Cheshire-cat grin, that he was happy now – deliriously so. My partner told me he had suffered with depression in his life and yet now, he was standing in front of me (in my mind's eye) perpetually smiling and laughing as I looked at him. It was infectious. You couldn't escape it. It seemed he was showing me that no matter what had happened and how he had felt when alive, he could not be happier than he was now, and he wanted his best friend to know this, and to be reassured and comforted by it. When we work together in our circle, it's often very emotional because we get such joy and comfort from the communication we receive from our dead loved ones in spirit, and we can feel the strength and power of their emotions - the love they still have for their family and friends, and very often we're brought to tears by it. We can feel how much they still care for us, and we can see that they still look out for us and follow our daily lives and know what we do every day. When we ask a spirit to 'blend' with us, we can feel the power of their love for a family member because their emotions flood into our body. It can literally take your breath away: It's love like you've never felt before.

Another night in our home circle we were practising 'speed reading' – like speed dating but giving psychic readings. I sat with a young lady who had recently joined our circle. I had only ever really said hello and goodbye to her; beyond that, I knew nothing about her, other than that her accent was not British. Again, I was asked to make contact with any deceased member of her family and tell her how they died. As I closed my eyes, I could see a sturdy outdoors-man, with a thick moustache and dark hair. He was standing near a river in the countryside, and then he took me to his house nearby. It seemed to be old, made of thick stone, and lacking in any modern appliances. I described the man to my partner, and she said this was her uncle. She asked me how he died and I instantly said, "With a shotgun – he was shot!" The words came out of my mouth so fast, and I could see the gun – but knew he had not committed suicide – he had been killed. My partner confirmed this was indeed the case. It was as though I had heard the words in my head. Sometimes I see the words, written like huge banners in front of me; but I have to point out, this is not because I'm good at it –I'm embarrassingly rubbish at it compared to the mediums in my home circle. But also, it's the spirits who do this, not me – they place the words for me to see, put the images and scenes into my head – it's not my ability – it's all theirs.

Proof of the Afterlife

But going back to the medium Dennis Barrett now, and as he continued to sit in his home circle, he also inadvertently progressed as a spiritual healer too, and one of his most dramatic healings, which was also among his first, happened when a local couple came with their baby to see him. They were in a state of desperation, and as soon as they arrived at Dennis' house, they naturally wanted to tell him what was wrong with the baby, but Dennis stopped them, telling them he didn't need or want to know. The couple, never having been to a 'healer' before, were rather disconcerted by this, but Dennis simply asked if he could hold the baby. For about half a minute he held the baby in his arms and then gave her back to the mother. "She's alright now," he told the parents. "I've done what I had to do..." He explains, 'I knew that everything was alright because my spirit helpers had put the words in my mouth. I just let them come out.' The parents were nonplussed and not a little irritated as they went to leave, and the husband insisted on telling Dennis about the medical condition their baby was suffering from. She had a contortion of the spine, he said, and doctors had told them it would only get worse and worse. It would twist her spine like a corkscrew. It was a condition called infantile scoliosis. She would never be able to walk or even sit up, he said. Nothing could be done to stop this. The following day, the parents had an appointment to see the specialist at hospital. He told them that all he could offer was physiotherapy, and that no other intervention would be possible. Feeling completely dejected, the parents agreed for the consultant to arrange their first physio appointment, which would take place the following week. When the parents arrived for their appointment, they waited and waited to be called into the physio's room. The physiotherapist kept coming out into the waiting room, looking around, then going back into the treatment room. Eventually, the physiotherapist asked the parents if they had seen anyone else arrive, to which the parents said, "No," but added that they were here to see her. The physiotherapist took one look at their baby and replied, "Your baby hasn't got infantile scoliosis!" The puzzled physiotherapist then phoned their consultant, who said he would see them all the next day to look into the situation. The following day, when the consultant examined the baby, he was just as puzzled as the physiotherapist. He told the parents, "Hmm, I could say this isn't the same baby since she no longer appears to have the condition she had last Friday..." X-rays were duly taken, which are displayed in Dennis' book, and the new X-rays showed that the baby no longer had a contorted spine at all; in contrast to the old x-rays which vividly showed the condition of her badly twisted spine. The baby went on to grow up into a perfectly healthy adult; you would never have known she had ever had such a terrible disability. The spirits, through Dennis, had healed her. Quite understandably, most people are going to naturally think that Dennis' tales of healing people through spirit intervention is simply incredulous; too fantastical to possibly be true – that this is the mind of a madman speaking and he is simply fabricating these stories; but it will get even wilder as this book progresses! I would have thought the same thing myself too – had I not experienced things so out of this world, so incomprehensibly mind blowing, when I was doing the research for this book.

One day, Dennis was riding his motorbike on his usual route home from work when he found himself wondering what would happen if one of his spirit helpers came through while he was riding his motorbike. 'As if answer to my thoughts, the bike seemed to shrink. It felt like a toy beneath my knees and I was looking down at the road from a distinctly elevated position.... Then I had a moment of panic. When would I return to normal size? A car was coming towards me. The driver looked across as we passed, and I heard the squeal of tyres as he accelerated away.' The motorist, quite understandably, had been terrified! Fortunately, gradually Dennis' size returned to normal. He describes this spirit in more detail; and just when you think it couldn't get any stranger, it does. Not long before the motorbike incident, Dennis had been carrying out a healing session, when all of a sudden, he felt a new spirit enter him. 'This one felt like a very large man. I work in my shirtsleeves without a tie, which was just as well because he turned out to be a Zulu… People in the hall saw me expand and grow. All the buttons of my shirt popped off, just like when David Banner turns into the Incredible Hulk!' That evening, Dennis went to his development circle as usual and he told them what had happened. His spirit guides must have heard him because they came through, 'saying that they too had found the incident amusing!' They told him, "It is important for you to realize that we can use every faculty you possess, every capability … all we need is the chance, the invitation." I've seen similar in the home circle I belong to, no-where near as dramatic as Dennis' experience, but the mediums' faces change in features, and a strange voice, not their own, will come out of them when they talk. One night while we were practicing going into trance and allowing a spirit to take over our bodies, I could feel as a spirit's face took over mine. I could feel that the skin on my face suddenly felt different. In my mind's eye, my fingers ran down my face and the texture felt much coarser and the shape of my face felt longer and narrower now. My tutor, sitting next to me said the shape of my cheek bones changed. Did I imagine this all? Well, it was very hard to concentrate at the time, because meanwhile, the medium sitting next to me, who is a relative beginner like myself, was completely taken over by a spirit. His body suddenly began to tremble violently and he began to speak in an entirely different voice to his own. It was the first time anything like this had happened to him. He said his name was "George," and that he was lost. He started to cry. His face was full of anguish, and his features were altering. I couldn't concentrate on my exercise any longer and abandoned it – I was too fascinated by what was happening and I had goose bumps watching it. It was mind-boggling, otherworldly, astonishing. The medium had no idea it was happening – he had gone so deep into trance. He's the most down - to - earth, regular man, with an ordinary job and family, and like most of us in the group, spends much of the time laughing at himself and our sometimes - failed efforts to communicate with spirits. Having got to know him and his wife, who sits in the circle too, all I can say is that they're the most genuine and humble people. He certainly would never have expected this to happen to him! And, if he had been faking it, our tutors would have sussed this out because, quite remarkably, they are able to 'link-in' and see, hear, and experience what we are experiencing clairvoyantly. Our tutor intervened and helped the lost spirit "George" find his way into the light where his family were waiting for him – he hadn't realized he was dead.

Well, going back to Dennis Barrett now and he adds, with his feet firmly on the ground too, that despite the unexpected events which kept occurring in his own development, 'There is no need to stand on ceremony with our spirit helpers. They are human like us and fallible like us… They are people, not ghosts.' This is quite an important point because when a spirit comes through to me, I'm often so shocked that it's happened that I'm like a rabbit caught in the headlights, and I flounder, urgently wondering to myself if I'm imagining it, or trying to think of something to say to them. Its shock and awe at the same time, and yet in actual fact, usually these spirits aren't Zulu warriors or ascended masters or angels – they're someone's father, mother, grandad, child; and they're just the same as you and I, with the same thoughts, emotions, concerns for their family, habits and hobbies; so put quite simply, we can talk to them when they come to us just like we would if they were still here. And, they still have the same sense of humour. It's great fun communicating with spirits; they love jokes. One day at my home circle we were having an open workshop and a couple of ladies came who we had never met before. We spent time in pairs, trying to get spirit communication from their loved ones for two minutes then moving to the next person and repeating the exercise. I sat with one of the women and tried to 'tune-in' to spirit, closing my eyes. Instantly, I saw a blonde lady with two blonde children in a red car, driving down a narrow street of houses in what I sensed was London but close to water. Well, I could see seagulls and it was almost like I could smell the sea or a river. The lady recognised the blonde lady as her dead sister-in-law.

Proof of the Afterlife

The car stopped outside a house which had a large round portal-style window in the attic. I described this all, and the lady told me that this had been her parents' house. Then, the most bizarre image flashed into my mind - so vividly. It was a giant yellow flapping fish! I thought to myself, "I can't tell her this! What on earth has a huge flapping fish got to do with anything!" I thought this had to simply be a graphic indication of the panic I was feeling myself because I was so rubbish at trying to be clairvoyant! However, with my tutor sitting right next to me, watching, encouraging me to just say what it was I was seeing, in the end I simply spouted it out, descending into giggles as I did so, but adding that I got the visual impression of a couple, who I sensed were her parents, showing me this fish. To my utter astonishment, and tremendous relief, the lady explained that she and all her siblings were allergic to fish and that her parents would tease them about this, and offer to cook them fish supper when they were alive; that it was a great family joke! What I got wrong was that I thought it was in London - yet I could also sense it was by the sea. As it turned out, the street was in the Docklands by the River Thames in London. What had seemed like meaningless madness to me, and a product of my own imagination; the giant fish, had turned out to be highly relevant, meaningful and sentimental to the lady receiving the message, despite how crazy I'd felt saying it to her. I had a somewhat similar experience when I attended an open circle at the SAGB, the Spiritual Association of Great Britain in London; a place where Sir Winston Churchill and Sir Arthur Conan Doyle were once members. As we sat in the circle, our task was to simply give whatever impressions we were receiving from spirit. I'd never been to the building before, and so the six or seven other people there that day were strangers to me. As I sat there, I thought I could see a man who looked like he was a fisherman, with a thick grey beard, a dark blue fisherman's cap and dark blue warm coat. But I had no idea who this man had come for or who he belonged to. Regardless, I was encouraged by the tutor to say what I was seeing and so I did, adding that I wasn't sure that this wasn't just a product of my own imagination, but the man sitting next to me said he recognised the description and believed it was his uncle in spirit, who had been a keen angler, and whose surname had been 'Fish.' The tutor then laughed and said to me, "Ah, that would explain why I kept seeing a giant fish behind you!" Much of the time in my home circle, we find ourselves laughing uncontrollably because of the things spirits do when they come to see us. They have a great sense of humour – just like they did when they were alive. Dennis Barrett is right; we don't need to stand on ceremony. At the SAGB one day recently, I was sitting in circle when I suddenly saw a man waving a blue and white football scarf above his head. I turned to one of the men in the circle and told him this, adding that I sensed it was his brother in spirit, although I didn't know if he had a brother, or if he did, whether the brother was dead or alive. I felt silly saying it too, because I also thought I had just imagined it, or my mind had simply made it up. Just before this, another man in the group had left the room to go to the bathroom. When he returned, he turned to the same man and said, "By the way, I've got a man here who's shaking a football rattle." The bathroom was not next door to the room we were in, it was on another floor, so it doesn't seem that he could have heard me.

CHAPTER THREE

'I was being prodded and poked and tickled – by invisible hands.'

Isa Northage died in 2002 at the age of 92. She too was a remarkable physical medium, who set up a healing sanctuary in the grounds of Newstead Abbey in Nottingham in the 1930's. Her daughter Hannah Carlin, nee Nina Northage says in the introduction to Isa's biography A Path Prepared, 'Growing up it seemed perfectly normal in our home to see objects move, to see the table we ate at rise… the Christmas tree with the spirit children materializing… From the beginning, through experiments with ectoplasm from which materializations built, I was there.' Allan MacDonald, who worked with Isa as one of her assistants, and subsequently wrote the biography with Isa, says that among the spirits who communicated through her were, 'Doctors, scientists, clergy and writers, bringing evidence of continuity of life.' But before all this began, one day in 1916, Isa had gone for a walk in the woods. She always used to go there with her fiancé, but he had gone off to fight in the War. She was feeling very lonely and sad, and she sat down for a while on a bench. All of a sudden, the forest scenery around her appeared to change into a battlefield, and soldiers on horseback rode into view. One of the soldiers was her fiancé. Suddenly, a rifle shot rang out, and she watched in horror as her fiancé fell from his horse. A soldier riding beside him shot at a German snipper, then dismounted and knelt beside her fiancé, comforting him, and not caring for his own safety. Isa knew in that moment that her fiancé had been mortally wounded. Gradually, the vision faded and Isa walked back home, devastated. She told her mother what had happened and her mother tried to reassure her, telling her to dismiss it all from her mind, but Isa knew in her heart that it was true. Shortly afterwards, formal paperwork arrived telling her that her fiancé had been granted leave, and requesting that she make arrangements for their upcoming marriage. Weeks passed by, and then in July another letter arrived, informing Isa that her fiancé had been killed in battle. Her vision had been tragically correct.

Isa joined the W.R.A.F. as a volunteer to help in the war effort on the home front, and in time, she met and married the soldier who had comforted her fiancé when he'd been fatally shot. Isa also formed a small orchestra to entertain people during the terrible trauma of the War. It was during this time that she began to see spirit people appearing. They would stand in front of her and the orchestra when she was on stage, telling her that they wished to speak, or requesting certain music to be played, and asking to give a message to their loved ones. The spirit appearances became so overwhelming that by 1937 Isa retired from the orchestra to focus on devoting her time to these 'visitors,' and word soon spread. One witness at a platform demonstration at the St Brotherhood Church in Pontypridd, Wales, later told a reporter for a spiritualist magazine of the day that a young dead soldier came through when Isa was in trance and he described his life and his death. The soldier explained that he had been shot in the hand. When Isa came out of trance at the end of the demonstration, 'Bullet wounds had produced clear marks on the hand of the medium in the exact place described by the dead soldier.' The magazine also describes a private sitting with Isa, where the wife of one of the guests 'materialized in full form,' and spoke. 'She kissed her husband on the forehead, the sound of the kiss being audible to all.' At another séance, a parrot manifested and flew about the room! Isa was levitated by the spirits on one occasion; her feet rising to the level of the sitter's heads. Mr. D. M. Antliff, who was present and representing Two Worlds magazine, reported that a nun materialised and placed a rosary on his knee, and whispered kind words to him. He later wrote, 'I clearly saw her lips moving, the movement of her eyes, and I could feel her breath.' After a different seance, a witness called Mr. W. Gillet wrote, 'My mother built up for me,' and he adds, 'Who cannot recognise his own mother?' At another seance, witness J. Ward asked aloud if spirit would write on a blank postcard which had been placed on the table. He later wrote to Two Worlds magazine to say, 'We saw a materialized hand float.' The hand then proceeded to write on the blank postcard. At the same séance, a number of spirit children also materialised, he said. They were mischievous and set-about ruffling-up a gentleman guest's hair, pulling his tie and tickling his legs, 'with yelps of delight.' While I haven't yet seen spirit children, I've been told by our home circle leaders that they were present one night when we were attempting 'table-tipping.' Sitting around a small circular table in the semi-darkness that night, we were all desperately trying to keep our hands as still as possible as we rested them very lightly on the table-top. An hour or so passed by and nothing happened. It was getting late and I was looking forward to going home to bed when suddenly I felt my hair being pulled, on one side of my head, then the other, then a sudden poke on my back and a tug on my blouse, then my hair again, and another poke on my shoulder. I could clearly see everyone else's hands were plainly still resting lightly on the top of the table. I was being prodded and poked and tickled – by invisible hands. One of the other ladies felt her long hair being pulled too. By this point, I couldn't stop giggling because of the tickling. In the dark, I couldn't see where they were going to poke me next! The spirit children were obviously having fun, and so was I!

But back to Isa Northage now, and at another of her séances, according to MacDonald, 'A bubbling mass of ectoplasm appeared in the centre of the room,' then 'a hand formed,' then, 'like a flash,' a spirit boy appeared. His mother, Mrs. S. Burrows was present, and she later wrote, 'My boy stood before us, smiling and full of life.' He'd been a sailor. His family were all at the séance, and the boy put his arm around his mother and spoke to his two brothers, she said. The spirits who most often physically appeared to Isa included a 'Dr. Reynolds,' who told her he had lived approximately one hundred and fifty years ago. Dr. Reynolds was the most frequent communicator, whose voice Isa could hear very clearly, but sometimes he showed himself physically to her too, appearing in the room with her when she treated patients who had come for healing. Isa had formed her own development circle, but she'd also established other circles across the country for the purpose of building up and drawing on all the sitters' energies, to help the spirits materialise physically; and then they got to work. 'It was this build-up of power,' Isa says, 'which led Dr Reynolds and his band of helpers from the spirit world to perform operations on mortal beings in cases such as cancer, tumour, ulcer etc, in some instances where they had been given up by medical men as being incurable.' Isa explains,

"There is a supernatural and spirit world in which human spirits, good and bad, live in a state of consciousness... death is only the beginning of a new and infinitely better life... we should not grieve because of their promotion." She did urge caution however, explaining that there were dangers to the medium during spirit materialisations; because ectoplasm 'emanating from the medium's body, which during trance is still an integral part of the physical body, could cause very serious bodily harm through shock and bring about haemorrhage and even death.' That's why physical mediums will say that stillness and calmness is required in the séance room by all participants; although that's not so easy when you're being tickled by hands you can't see!

Isa, or rather, Dr. Reynolds, performed "psychic surgery," and she admits that to those unfamiliar with this phenomenon, "This statement will doubtless sound very much like a flight of fancy, but I can assure you that the incidents I am about to relate did actually take place and there are many to bear witness to them." In one such incident, a "spirit operation" was performed by the dead Dr. Reynolds on a boy of 14. The boy had an inoperable brain tumour, and his parents had been told by Doctors that a cure was impossible and that there was nothing more that could be done for him. His eyesight was failing now too, as a result of the tumour. His mother had heard about Isa and brought her son to the healing sanctuary in the grounds of the Abbey. The boy's mother chose to sit outside the healing room, but her friend went inside with the boy, where Isa had three assistants and one lady whose job it was to keep records. As the healing session began, Isa closed her eyes and went into trance, and under the glow of a red light, 'Dr Reynolds materialized throughout the entire operation … his hands were clearly seen during the whole period, except for those moments when they sank into the patient's head.' Dr. Reynolds was apparently not alone that day – he told Isa there were other doctors in spirit assisting him too, and by the end of the procedure, Dr. Reynolds announced that they had killed the tumour; it would not grow again. The boy's eyesight would get better now too, he said. Dr. Reynolds then said that a fellow Doctor-in-spirit was going to say a few words, and suddenly, 'A trumpet standing on the floor was seen to rise,' From it came a voice, "This is Hollander. I was a brain specialist on earth… Everything will be alright now, and so will the eyes." Both doctors then said David should return in a few months, at which time they would physically remove the dead material of the tumour by performing another operation. When the appointed time came, 'The dead and shrivelled tumour was removed from David's head.' It was placed on swabs with Doctor Reynolds instructing that it should be burnt. 'The matter had a most obnoxious smell,' Isa says. Doctor Reynolds then 'showed himself in strong red light,' and the patient, David, 'was able to shake hands with him.' There were many more patients too who were helped by Dr. Reynolds and his team, including those who had been declared "incurable" with cancer. Here's an excerpt from an article in Two Worlds Magazine in 1939 by D.M. Antliff, who writes, 'One of the most valuable phases of mediumship is that of healing the sick, and I would like to relate some of the remarkable cures which are being effected through the mediumship of Mrs. Northage; Patient has had removed a cancer of long standing... Most of the cases treated have been considered difficult; in fact, some have been declared incurable by the medical faculty. Mrs. Northage's guide, Dr. Reynolds, speaks to his healers and patients... He will often talk for half an hour, the sitters asking questions, to which he replies freely. He will diagnose each case and give details as to its exact nature.' As to the veracity of accounts, Antliff writes, 'One has only to converse with the patients at this centre to be assured of remarkable evidence concerning the work being done.'

Maurice Barbanell, former editor of Psychic News writes, 'Her spirit doctor materialises, Dr. Reynolds, who says he practised on earth about 150 years ago, and publicly performs these bloodless operations... He states he is helped by other former members of the medical profession who had expressed the desire to utilise their combined earthly experience and spirit knowledge to help the suffering... I have many accounts of these painless and successful spirit operations... Ernest Thompson,' (former editor of Two Worlds) 'has recorded in detail an operation he witnessed; he was allowed to take away with him one of the ulcers which had been removed from a patient. He had this analysed under a microscope in a laboratory by a medical expert. The analyst later reported that it was an acute duodenal ulcer, its condition showing that it was about to penetrate the intestine and would have proved fatal at an early date.' In another of Isa's many patients, she writes, 'A case of chronic asthma was uniquely healed by Dr. Reynolds, fully materialised to the helpers and sitter.' To achieve this Dr. Reynolds, 'Proceeded to remove the mucus from the chest by inserting his de-materialized hand and taking away the matter in long strands, the filth being deposited in a kidney tray.' It had a 'pungent and offensive smell,' Isa noted!

When Isa was alive and carrying out her "psychic surgery," she would often be contacted by doctors and surgeons at hospitals in England, asking for her help. 'The spirit doctors keep close observation on hospitals and surgeries; they know all the most up to date treatments,' she says. She explains that lots of healing was also carried out by the doctor and his spirit team using absent or distant healing, 'by the power of prayer and concentration,' when patients were not well enough to make the visit to her sanctuary. A Mrs. Fisher provided her testimony of how she was healed by Isa's spirit doctors. She says she also witnessed the appearance of a 'dead' person. "My mother-in-law started to build up right in between my husband and myself, I would say within a foot of us… The ectoplasm seemed to start on the floor and gradually rose to the height of six feet, and out of this pillar, my mother-in-law emerged." A Mr. W. Molson of Grimsby also wrote his account. He had never met Isa Northage before the day of the séance. As he sat with her, Dr. Reynolds 'Appeared, fully materialised.' Mr. Molson says, 'He chatted to me just as any doctor would chat with a patient in his consulting room, taking my head in his materialised hands and examining it.' The spirit doctor's fingers, 'were as normal and natural as the touch of any human hand,' according to Mr. Molson, who also saw his deceased mother too. 'She appeared beside me fully materialised.'

CHAPTER FOUR

'The spirit girl weighed 77 lbs.'

Back further in time now, and in the 1890's in Boston, America, Edward Brackett was a sculptor and conservationist, maintaining species of flowers and shrubs. He became involved in the scientific breeding of species of fish, and was appointed the supervisor of inland fisheries. He sculpted the bust of John Brown, a leading martyr in the abolition of slavery, before Brown was executed. He also set out to investigate spirit materialisations, and he would go on to write the book, Materialised Apparitions: If not beings from another life, what are they? When Brackett began his explorations, he believed that being a sculptor would enable him 'to detect the slightest differences between objects,' and he emphasised; 'I have an abhorrence of fraud,' which he was determined to root out during his investigations. Unfortunately, no matter how scrupulous Brackett set out to be, he was fooled on one occasion, for it was around this time that an anonymous writer had also set out to expose trickery within seances, which was often flagrant yet ingeniously deceptive; for there was money to be made in seances, at the expense of the most vulnerable, who in their grief were desperate to be reunited with their dead loved-ones. The anonymous writer published a pamphlet with a rather strange title. It was called, Some account of the Vampires of Onset, and it had the intention of unmasking some of the popular mediums of the day in Massachusetts. Onset is a town in Massachusetts, and presumably, the writer is referring not to literal vampires, but rather, to the leeches of fake mediums who were active there at the time. They say, 'The compiler of this little pamphlet is not an opponent of spiritualism; on the contrary, he has for many years been interested in the study of psychical phenomena.' However, he became determined to expose 'the vile creatures who, under the mask of mediumship, have been coining money from the most sacred feelings of the human heart… to victimize and demoralize heart-broken mourners seeking knowledge of their beloved dead.' The writer did not appear to be alone in their sentiment. 'That such vermin are permitted among people claiming to be civilized and respectable, is a matter of profound astonishment to a large number of spiritualists.' One such medium the writer investigated was called Mrs. Cowan, who Brackett, the sculptor, also sat with. Fortunately, Brackett did not include Mrs. Cowan in his book as a medium he could vouch for, and he had apparently been furious when he learned of the medium's tricks. 'The Vampires of Onsett' describes how Mrs. Cowan came to be caught out when a young lady confessed to a Boston Herald Newspaper reporter that clever deception had been used at Mrs. Cowan's seances. The young lady told the reporter that she herself was very poor, and one day she was introduced by another lady to the possibility of some fruitful earnings if she pretended to be a materialised dead person at a séance. Mrs Cowan and her husband then visited her, she explained, and told her how she could help them. The young lady says she then made visits to the Cowan's house on several occasions to attend rehearsals. "The salary they offered was in excess of what I could possibly earn in my chosen occupation, and I was induced to take up the business," she explained to the reporter. "The spirit, when inexperienced, usually receives $1 for each séance," she said. "Mrs. Rich," another imposter, "was paid $3 a seance, and this is the highest price I ever knew to be paid for a single seance. I should say that $1.50 is a pretty fair price for playing spirit." The young lady said her role was to replace the more experienced spirit impersonator, Mrs. Florence K. Rich, "who was a performer of such ability in this line as to make her services in great demand in other cabinets, her salary being double that of others in the same business." It would appear then that it was not just Mrs Cowan's seances where trickery was carried out. The first time the young lady worked at a séance held by Mrs Cowan's, "It was at an afternoon seance. Mrs. Rich, in the garb of a spirit, led me from the cabinet as another visitor from the unseen world… I advanced to where Dr. Whitney and his wife were sitting, and represented myself as their dead daughter Ethel." She worked alongside several other impersonators too, she explained. "The male spirits were personated by Mr. Cowan's brother Andrew, while Mrs. Cowan and I played the role of female spirits, each having our signals for entrances and exits." She explained how she and the other impersonators hid from the audience; "In the rear of the cabinet used by the Cowan's was a door leading into a room which the "spirits" used as their headquarters. This door had been locked with a great show of sincerity, and the key handed to someone in the circle for safe keeping." However, what the audience did not know was that the Cowan's had a stick which could be inserted into the casing of the lock of the door to open it for the spirit impersonators who "could noiselessly enter the cabinet amid the singing circle and noise of the cabinet organ." The spirit impersonators each wore white robes that were "shrouded in black cambric while passing from the room into the cabinet, thus rendering them invisible in the dim light of the seance room." A secret hiding place for the impersonators was also available, "after Mr Cowan removed the floor of a bay window and placed the cabinet in that location." Yet, "To all appearances, this cabinet was fraud-proof. A trap-door had been placed in the floor by which means the 'spirits' could enter from the cellar." Mr. Cowan had discovered a large space under the floor that did not directly connect with the cellar itself – so that if the cellar were searched, the hiding space above it would not be found, the young lady explained. "Business went on prosperously," she says. At some of the seances that Mr. Brackett attended, she claims, "I personated his niece Bertha, whom he desired to see on every occasion, always calling him "uncle," and grasping him by the hand and leading him up to the cabinet for whisperings with the 'spirits,' and how Mr. Brackett would express great delight at seeing me." She explains how she managed to fool him; "I would materialize for Mr. Brackett at the back of his chair, or in some remote part of the room. In order to do this, it was necessary for me to creep behind the black curtain that hung around the wall, counting the chairs by feeling as I crept along, until I came to the one occupied by Mr. Brackett. I would then jump up and greet him…and take him by the hand." She was not the only 'spirit' to fool Brackett, she claims; "Andy always personated Mr. Brackett's dead brother George, and we were often greatly amused by his enthusiastic descriptions of our seances." The young lady goes on to explain other deceptions carried out upon sitters. "A Mr. Russel of Cambridgeport was very anxious to see his "three darlings," as he designated his two deceased wives and his intended third." However, at this séance, only the young lady herself and the medium were present. "How do you suppose we managed it?" she asks the reporter without waiting for a reply. "It was very simple.... we merely rigged up Andy in female apparel. Andy was a little shaky, however, having positively refused to sacrifice his moustache; and so, the excuse was invariably offered that the spirit was never 'strong' enough to get very far away from the cabinet. We had many a laugh over Andy's nervousness while wearing petticoats!" She and her fellow impersonators found it all rather good fun.

In another pamphlet titled, Notes from Boston: Startling Evidence of the Deception Practised by Materializing Mediums, written by a person using the pseudonym Guilluame, the fraud in Massachusetts is further exposed thanks to a Mr. John Curtis, who was a retired clothing business owner. Mr. Curtis was a wealthy man and he resided at the Clarendon Hotel. In April 1888, he invited a number of people to go to his hotel apartment where he showed them a large array of wigs, clothes, mosquito netting, cork stilts, moustaches, white shawls and more 'which had been captured, mainly by Mr. Curtis, in the frequent exposures of the Boston mediums.' Guilluame writes particularly of a recurring "spirit child." 'Little Elsie was never known to advance into the circle for the best of reasons. The young woman who personated her was upon her knees and was attired in a short child's frock.' As a result of his expose, Guilluame revealed that Mr. Curtis 'has received a number of anonymous letters threatening him with bodily injury, and one writer went so far as to intimate an assassination probable;' but Mr. Curtis said he was not frightened!

It's important to include accounts like this because trickery certainly did happen, both then and still now. Although physical mediumship is exceptionally rare these days, a medium called Gary Mannion was captured on infra-red video in 2016, at a séance in Essex, England, masquerading in the dark as a dead person. When the lights of the séance room were turned back on, Mannion was seen to have freed himself from the ties binding his arms and legs to his chair, and was wandering around the room, breathing on the sitters and touching them, pretending to be a materialised spirit. Unfortunately for him, someone there had sneaked a video recorder into the room, and the footage of Mannion's charade went viral in spiritualist circles. Sadly, behaviour like this sets the movement back enormously, making it a laughing stock, and it simply gives ammunition to the many sceptics. In the Victorian era, some photographs of supposedly materialised dead people were actually cut-outs of faces from newspapers! Interestingly, when mentioning the more recent Gary Mannion debacle to my home circle tutors, imagine my surprise when they told me they had actually been there at the time, having paid to go and see it, and that one of them had turned to the other in the dark and said, "This isn't right." They had known mediumistically that all was not as it should be, that it was not the real deal. And, the moral of the story is never try to kid a real medium, because they will know! Curiously, one of my tutors did add that they believed Mannion did have some genuine mediumistic abilities; but he'd ruined all that now. He was cast-out of the community with his reputation deservedly ruined. Presumably, his ego had got the better of him and he'd set out to prove he was the best medium out there – the one out of so very few who can produce real genuine physical materialisations of spirits. He'd thought he could fool people. Instead, his reputation was left in tatters. Perhaps it should be said here, as spiritual investigator Henry Steel Olcott once pointed out back in the 1800's; "I am not, I am happy to say, that class of pseudo-investigators which rejects the chance of finding truth in these marvels because mediums occasionally cheat. It has often and justly been said that the circulation of counterfeit coins is no proof that the genuine does not exist." Con-artists exist in all professions, and mediumship is just one of them. Fortunately, it seems that Edward Brackett became aware of the trickery used on him at some of these seances, and as a result, he did not write about them in his book Materialised Beings, for he quite naturally dismissed them as chicanery. He does comment that at one séance, 'What was claimed by the manager to be Bertha came out….and in honestly relating what has come to me at these séances,

I am forced to state that the form that appeared on this occasion was not Bertha, and that there was, as subsequent events proved, an attempt to deceive me.' Brackett rumbled the impersonation, and says rather dramatically of the medium, 'Mrs. Sawyer is a gentlewoman and a strong medium, but she is surrounded by a coarse magnetism, the baleful influence of which she seems powerless to resist.'

Brackett also describes attending a séance by the medium Mrs. Fay, along with approximately thirty other people. Before it begins, the lighting is lowered, but Brackett says 'not so low that we could not discern clearly the features of those around us.' During the séance, Brackett said his late wife materialised – although he noted that she didn't look identical to how he had known her. He said he held onto her hand and as he let go, 'she went down directly in front of me, within a foot of where I stood, her head and shoulders being the last part visible.' On the carpet where she disappeared, there was 'a glow of phosphorescent light, which gradually faded.' If this is the case, it surely doesn't seem possible that a trickster, impersonating a spirit, could be lifting up a trap door and crawling inside of it in this instance – for surely the awkward movements of their body would have been seen, by both Brackett and all the other onlookers? And how could an impersonator disintegrate before his eyes, literally vanishing in front of them all, by trickery?

On his way home however, Brackett could not stop thinking that he had been deceived, and he felt rather annoyed. He became determined to investigate further. "If I could only get the inside track," he thought, "how easy it would be to expose it!" So, he resolved to attend more seances. At the very next seance, 'The forms were coming quite freely to me,' he writes, and the control spirit greeted him personally; 'I had my arm around the waist of the form that took me right into the cabinet.' Once inside the cabinet, he says, 'With my right hand I reached out and satisfied myself that the medium was sitting in the chair,' and he concludes, 'There could be no mistake - there were four of us in the cabinet; the two forms that appeared to be materialised, the medium, and myself! I know how two got in, but where did the other two come from?' Brackett set out to thoroughly search the cabinet. He had it pulled out, and examined thoroughly 'the floor, wall and everything connected with it,' but he found no trickery. 'There was no chance for confederates to be used here - it was impossible for anyone to enter the cabinet except through the door of the séance room, in the presence of the whole audience.' Even so, he asked to be seated right next to the cabinet, 'which place I occupied for about 40 sittings,' he says. Having sat in forty further seances, Brackett concludes, 'I know it is impossible to use a confederate in this cabinet without its being detected.' His deceased wife appeared to him many times during these seances. If this was an imposter, why was it that Brackett says, 'The likeness was so marked; that it would have been impossible to mistake it.' The spirit looked so much like his wife that he felt no confusion about it this time. He also describes other spirits that appeared too. 'I have seen a tall young man, wearing a full beard, claiming to be the brother of a lady with me.' The lady however did not recognise her brother, telling him that he was just a boy when she knew him.' Here then is a perfect example of a living person impersonating a spirit, isn't it? And yet, Brackett continues, 'At this, the spirit figure stooped, kissed her on the cheek,' and, 'raised his face to hers without the beard,' while 'at the same time, diminishing in size until he was more nearly the boy she knew.' The spirit had changed in shape and size right before their eyes. If this was simply explained as a person pretending to be a spirit and getting down on their knees, wouldn't Brackett and all the sitters have seen the person do this, when it was light enough in the room to see, and when they were all watching so avidly? So again, how could this have been an imposter? The same medium Mrs. Fay is also discussed in There is No Death, by Florence Marryat in 1891. Mrs H. B. Fay was a materialisation medium from Boston. Mrs. Marryat estimates that during the séance she attended, she saw between 30 to 40 different materialised forms, including mothers and babies, and Marryat's own deceased brother Frederick, who had drowned at sea.

Meanwhile, Brackett continued in his investigations, sitting in a séance with a medium called Mrs Fairchild, who unlike most mediums, did not sit in a cabinet but sat outside of it. 'Thus,' Brackett says, 'eliminating from her seances all chance of transfiguration or impersonation by the medium.' It was a private séance, and he was accompanied by his friend William D. Brewer. Brackett examined the cabinet beforehand, even though Mrs Fairchild sat outside of it. The séance lasted about two hours, 'During which time scarcely a minute passed that there were not forms out in the room...Sometimes three or four at once,' says Brackett. 'As I examined the walls and everything connected with the temporary cabinet, I have no hesitation in saying that the forms that came from or appeared in it were materialised beings. I was in this cabinet several times during the séance, often with two (spirits) forming at the same time. Once I sat between them, an arm around each.'

At another seance, Brackett says his niece appeared, 'Stretching out her bare arms,' and 'turning them that everyone could see that there was nothing in them. She brought the palms of her hands together, rubbing them as if rolling something between them. Very soon there descended from her hands a substance which looked like lace.' She continued her hand movements, 'til several yards of it lay upon the carpet.' She asked her uncle Brackett to kneel, telling him he was "too tall," and then 'she proceeded to make a robe around me.' The robe had no sleeves, 'so she took each arm in turn and materialised sleeves.' Then, she told her uncle, "You have not enough hair," and upon rubbing her hands over his head, 'materialised a wig!' The control spirit, "Emma," came out of the cabinet wearing a white satin dress. Mr. Whitlock, a close friend of Mr Brackett, who was also present, asked the spirit Emma if he might be allowed to cut a piece of her dress. She agreed that he could, and a small piece was snipped, leaving a noticeable hole in the dress. However, 'the damage seemed to be soon repaired.' Somehow, the hole in the dress had simply vanished, and the dress was perfect again. Another spirit appeared, claiming to be 'a German chemist,' who 'Magnetized or medicated a tumbler of water with sparks of light flashing freely from his fingers into the water.' There was also the appearance of a spirit called Dr. J. R. Newton, 'The widely known healer, some- time deceased.' Brackett and Whitlock, who had known Doctor Newton, greeted him. 'I shook hands with him,' says Brackett, 'and had time to study his face well; there could be no mistake; it was a wonderful likeness of the doctor.' Brackett's friend Mr. Whitlock, who was the editor of Facts Magazine, saw his dead father materialise, and both he and his wife, who was also present, confirmed the likeness. Whitlock's written statement includes, 'My father, Rev. Geo. C. Whitlock, LLD, who passed to spirit-life about twenty years ago, was perfectly materialised.' With regards to cutting the spirit "Emma's" dress, he explains, 'While I was kneeling before the form, the hole which I had made in the dress did disappear, and that I used my senses of both sight and feeling to convince myself of the facts.' He adds that at this seance, 'Over 60 forms appeared, most of whom were recognised.' How could they all have been impersonators, yet able to look so much like these "dead" friends and relatives, and be so recognisable? How could the impersonators have known what all these relatives had looked like and managed to ensure they were identical in appearance to them? It doesn't seem possible that this was trickery. Brackett also describes how the control spirit, Emma, 'Dematerialised directly in front of me, so near that I could have laid my hands upon her as she went down.'

After another séance, with an audience of twenty-five people, Brackett concludes, 'To suppose that the twenty-five honest, intelligent persons who witnessed this were deceived, or that the appearance of the form was due to a confederate, is simply absurd.' No cheating was possible, he believed, particularly given that he had been inside the cabinet himself when the spirits materialised.

CHAPTER FIVE

'The spirit man took a seat on the music stool and proceeded to play half a dozen perfectly harmonious chords, using both hands.'

Robert Gambier Bolton, born in 1854, was the official photographer of Queen Victoria's animals. He was an English anthropologist, naturalist and photographer of natural history. His photography is still sought after by collectors, and some of his pictures are on display in the Natural History Museum. He was a Fellow of the Royal Geographic Society and a Fellow of the Zoological Society. He was also the author of Ghosts in Solid Form: An investigation of a certain little-known phenomena: Materializations. His book was the result of carrying out a series of experiments over 7 years, which resulted, rather astonishingly, in multiple manifestations of 'dead' people; though it was not without its dangers. Gambier writes, 'I have been permitted to examine the sensitive (here he means 'the medium,') at the moment when an entity, clad in a fully-formed temporary body, was walking amongst the experimenters, and the distorted features, the shrivelled-up limbs and contorted trunk of the sensitive at that moment proclaimed the danger connected with the production of this special form of phenomena.' According to Gambier, the medium's body and face had entirely changed, from healthy and vibrant to 'shrivelled up' and 'distorted,' as the materialised spirit took energy from the body of the medium, leaving him withered and depleted. As is still the case, Gambier admits that materialisation mediums are exceptionally rare, and these days only a handful across the world seem to genuinely exist. Of course, there has been fakery by unscrupulous con-artists, as there will always be, and through the ages they have been unceremoniously exposed and their reputations deservedly ruined; but Gambier was wise to this possibility, and he insists that he rigidly guarded against this in his experiments, by putting in place a number of measures including checking for secret hidden doors or mirrors in the rooms that were used. In fact, for Experiment One, he went to rather extreme lengths to avoid any possibility of being fooled, by conducting the experiment in a caravan in the middle of a forest, in the middle of the night! This was, says Gambier, 'A simple but exceedingly severe test.' The location was the middle of Lyndhurst Forest in Hampshire, and the medium was virtually blind! He was a man in his 40's, who Gambier says, 'Was taken by us on a dark night to a spot totally unknown to him, as he had only just arrived from London by train.' The medium was taken inside a 'large travelling caravan, which he had never been before.' Gambier had purchased the caravan the day before from a builder, and earlier in the day, he'd made a thorough examination inside it, 'To satisfy myself that no one was or could possibly be concealed in it.' He'd then locked the caravan up and put the key in his pocket, where it remained until they returned with the medium that night.

As they reached the caravan, amid the complete black-out of the swath of trees in the forest, Gambier locked them inside. This test, he said, would be extremely difficult because the conditions 'we considered as so utterly bad as to make failure a certainty.' There wasn't even a comfortable chair for the medium to be seated in, there was no soft music to create a conducive atmosphere, as is usually the case in seances, and no audience of sitters to lend their energy to the medium. Astonishingly however, within a quarter of an hour, 'The figure of a tall man stood before us, a man so tall that he was compelled to bow his head.' The partition in the ceiling of the caravan above him was six foot high. The 'man' then began to speak, giving his rank as Colonel and telling them he had been killed in Egypt. During his life, he told them, he was deeply interested in materialisation, and he had come, he said, "To prove to you that I am not the sensitive masquerading before you... Stand close to me and so settle the matter." Gambier immediately moved toward the tall figure and stood alongside him, 'almost touching him,' and Gambier discovered that the spirit's features were completely unlike that of the blind medium. 'The man 'towered above me, four inches taller than the sensitive.' After a few minutes, the figure disappeared, only to be replaced by a new spirit! 'A slightly built younger man,' who was smaller in height, and claiming to be 'a recently deceased member of the Royalty.' The spirit asked them to deliver a message to his mother, the Queen. At this point, Gambier's notes on this first experiment end, swiftly followed by his description of Experiment number Two, which, in contrast took place in Peckham, South East London, on a summer's day in July. The same blind medium was used again. Gambier points out that the conditions were far from ideal again – bright sunlight streamed into the room around the edges of the window blinds; yet in spite of this 'utterly hopeless' situation, again a figure appeared in the room. He stood beside the medium, then 'walked out into the room and stood between us, talking to us in a deep rich voice.' At the same time, 'We could hear the sensitive twelve feet away, moving uneasily on his chair and groaning.' In another of his experiments, Gambier used a medium who, rather than sitting enclosed in a cabinet, sat out among the small group of sitters, and like them, was able to watch as 'the materialized forms' build up beside him, 'talking to and with them during the process.' Most of Gambier's mediums went into trance, but this one appeared to have the ability to enable materialisations without needing to do so. Two of the sitters who were present told Gambier after the séance that they could see a 'thin white mist or vapor,' coming from the left side of the sensitive 'which passes into the sitter nearest to the sensitive... it then passes from sitter 1 to sitter 2 and so on until it has gone through the whole of the 16 sitters,' until it reaches the sensitive again, 'and disappears into his right side.' Gambier writes, 'We assume from this that the "power" – call it what you will – necessary for the formation of one of these temporary bodies, starts from the sensitive, passes through each sitter, drawing from each.' At this séance, there were two 'note takers,' who both later agreed they saw 'a white soft, dough-like substance.' Gambier writes, 'It seems to rest on the floor, somewhere near the right side of the sensitive.' This mysterious substance 'increases in bulk and commences to pulsate and move up and down, swaying as it grows in height.' Then, 'the entity quickly sets to work to mould the mass into something resembling a human body, commencing with the head. The rest of the upper portion of the body soon follows.' The legs and the feet come last, Gambier says. The spirit is then 'able to walk amongst the sitters.' The two note takers were in consensus when they observed that at all times, 'a thin band of the dough-like substance can be plainly seen issuing from the side of the sensitive, and joined onto the centre of the body inhabited by the entity.' When the spirits materialise, Gambier touches them, and on handling different portions of the materialized body, 'The flesh is found to be both warm and firm. The hands, arms, legs and feet are quite perfect.' He has, he says, taken a very detailed look at these materialised spirits, scrutinizing them 'at close quarters carefully,' and Gambier notes, 'In my opinion every materialisation has appeared to be at least 1/3 smaller (except as regards to height) than those possessed by beings on earth.' Gambier also claims to have seen materialized babies and infants. Some spirits, he says, have come through aged as they were in life, before they died, 'showing all the characteristics of old age – for the purpose of identification by the sitters – as they tell us. But we have seen materialized infants also; and on one occasion two still-born children appeared in our midst simultaneously – one showing distinct traces on its little face of a hideous deformity which it possessed at the time of its premature birth – a deformity known only to the mother who happened to be present that evening.' Gambier points out here, 'We are told that for the purpose of identification the entity will return to earth in an exact counterpart of the body which he alleges that he occupied at the time of his death in order that he may be recognised by his relatives and friends. The one who had lost a limb during his earth-life will return minus that limb.' But, Gambier adds, 'As soon as the identification has been established successfully, all this changes instantly; the four limbs will be seen,' and the spirit 'will henceforth show themselves to us in the very prime of life.' He says the spirits tell him emphatically that they are 'just as they really look and feel in the sphere which they now exist.' One guest at Gambier's seances was a ship's doctor, 'Who, although the fact was quite unknown to us – proved to be an expert linguist.' This became apparent after the medium began to speak in seven different foreign languages – though the medium 'had never in his life been out of England,' and who was 'conclusively proven to know no other language than English.' The ship's doctor conversed with spirits in French, German, Russian, Chinese and Japanese, and even, 'in the language of one of the hill-tribes of India.' In another perhaps quite comical session, Parsee guests from India were present. For the entire duration of the session, the spirits 'carried on their conversations in Hindustani,' and a heated debate broke out between the Indian visitors and two spirits who had materialised, 'over the disposal of the bodies of their dead, the entities insisting upon cremation…. The noise they made during this session being almost deafening.'

Gambier used a series of six mediums during his experiments, and his reports on the results are, he believes, 'sufficient to prove that we who have witnessed these marvels are neither hallucinated, insane, nor liars when we solemnly affirm that we have both seen and handled the materialised bodies.' For Experiment number Five, this seance took place at Gambier's own home in London where 'a tall and particularly graceful woman' materialised, who was seen visibly walking amongst the sitters, talking to them, and showing them her hands, 'the fingers being unusually long and tapering.' Experiment Six took place at the Psychological Society in London. The medium sat among the sitters, not using a cabinet. The two sitters on either side of the medium held his hands in theirs. They were the President and Vice President of the Psychological Society. A voice began to be heard, 'distinctly audible' to all of the guests, of which there were fourteen. Two men had also been posted outside the door to act as security, ensuring that no-one surreptitiously entered the room, and they both later confirmed hearing the spirit voice too. Soon, a spirit appeared, 'A slender man,' who 'after passing mysteriously through or over the circle formed by the sitters walked slowly to the harmonium.' The spirit man took a seat on the music stool and proceeded to play 'half a dozen perfectly harmonious chords,' using both hands, while 'working the pedals with both feet.' While this was happening, the medium was 'held securely during the whole time,' at a distance of twenty feet from the music stool. After about half an hour, the spirit man left the room and another figure appeared. This spirit apparently suggested that the harmonium should be played again, so Gambier himself got up, sat at the harmonium and began to play. Suddenly, the medium said to Gambier, "Look behind you please!" to which Gambier turned his head, and, 'almost touching me, stood the same tall and slender figure of a man.' Gambier stared closely at the spirit man's face, and observed that his features were 'distinctly different' to those of the medium, as well as being several inches taller too, thus ensuring that this was not the medium impersonating the spirit figure.

Experiment Seven took place in Whitehall, London, home to British politicians, where a male medium was taken to a very plush office. The seance had been arranged at the request of two young acquaintances of Gambier. He purposely doesn't give their names but says that they hold 'positions of State' and 'have never allowed the fact to leak out.' In their line of work, it would not have been seemly for it to have become known that they were communing with the dead, and they kept the séance a secret, not wishing to jeopardise their careers by admitting to such things. The visiting medium, Gambier says, had never been to this building before. As the séance began, 'The figure of a tall elderly man appeared, who stooped slightly as he walked.' He claimed to be a Lord who had served in the British Government, and he was, says Gambier, recognized by all the men present. Then, two more spirits appeared in human form, as well as 'a small animal from India!' And again, it becomes rather comical, as Gambier writes, 'In spite of my imploring the entities not to let him do so, or at least to keep him in check in such a palatial apartment… this the entities declared incapable of doing.' The materialised spirit creature apparently climbed onto the expensive writing-desk and scurried around madly, resulting in all the paperwork and pens being scattered everywhere in the ensuring mayhem! In another dramatic experiment, a female spirit appeared, who then 'dematerialised gradually like the Cheshire cat!' In this case, the male medium was seated in a corner of the room and 'wedged in there tightly by the ring of sitters grouped around him.' The female spirit 'walked out amongst the sitters and stood talking to them for about five minutes.' At the same time, one of the legs of the wooden chair the medium was sitting on 'suddenly gave way, and he fell forward into my arms!' Fortunately, Gambier was sitting next to him. 'The entity was not nearly so startled as the sitters,' he adds. When this spirit left, it passed, 'to all appearances through the floor.' This seems to be a common feature of materialisation, because many other mediums and sitters have witnessed the same thing, and perhaps this is the strongest argument against any trickery being carried out – because someone impersonating a spirit simply cannot disappear into nothingness by sinking into the floor!

Gambier's final experiment, number Nine, took place in Eaton Square, London with a male medium. 'Manifestations of both beasts and birds sometimes appeared,' wrote Gambier in his detailed records. 'The most startling being that of a deceased seal,' which apparently 'stayed long enough to tear some lace.' The lace was on the dress of a female guest. After the astonishing appearance of the seal, 'A medical man,' who was also present, made careful inspection of the lace that had been torn, while everyone else was instructed to remain in their seats. The medical man, a doctor, reported that there were, 'five green-coloured hairs hanging in the torn lace,' which 'had evidently become detached from the little animal's leg.' A naturalist friend of Gambier was also present, and he confirmed that, having often handled seals in his profession, these hairs did indeed appear to be seal hairs. They were wrapped in tissue paper and then placed inside a damp-proof and light-tight box. Strangely however, 'After a few days they commenced to dwindle in size and finally disappeared entirely.' Gambier adds, 'It was those five little hairs which settled the sneers of our would-be critics.' The same thing happened to any material that manifested during the seances; they would be collected in the same type of box, yet 'the material has always decreased in size, eventually disappearing…'

Curiously, Gambier says, 'It has been proved by means of a self-registering weighing machine on which he was seated, that the actual loss in weight to the sensitive, (the medium), when a fully materialised entity was standing in our midst, was no less than 65 pounds!'

CHAPTER SIX

"The eyes, and my God, the eyelids are moving!"

The medium Harry Edwards, much like almost every top-ranked medium throughout time, was a reluctant spiritualist. He didn't believe in all that mumbo-jumbo; yet, before long, he would end up on a stage at the Royal Albert Hall in London in front of audiences in their thousands, giving the most accurate messages from the spirit world to people who had come to see him. Harry Edwards was born to very ordinary working-class beginnings in Balham, London, in 1893, and despite going on to become perhaps the most famous medium in England, he certainly did not believe in so-called "mediums" when he was growing up. His father was a printer and his mother had been a dressmaker. Edwards was one of nine children, and according to his biographer, he was 'a holy terror' as a child, and often up to high jinks, which apparently included causing the derailment of railway trucks near the family home in Wood Green, and unofficially releasing a hot-air balloon at Alexandra Palace! He was also in the habit of mimicking the so-called "spirit guides" that mediums claimed they had, making his two sisters roll with laughter. His sisters were frequent visitors to a local Spiritualist Church, and when they came home at night, they would tell him all about the things that happened there. In response, Edwards would impersonate the mediums. He found it a jolly good laugh and all rather silly. However, as he grew older, he found himself being invited by some friends to go with them to a different Spiritual Church. This time, he readily accepted the invitation, excitedly anticipating his opportunity to expose the charlatan mediums there. Unfortunately for Edwards, the medium on the platform that night gave several very specific and highly accurate messages to him, about things she could not possibly have known about him. This shook Edwards; for he had been intent on exposing the gigantic fraud going on within spiritualism; that it was all nonsense and nobody could talk to the dead. Edwards carefully considered the possibility that collusion and pre-planning had to be behind what had happened; but he also considered that for the medium to be able to give such startlingly accurate evidence to so many people in the audience that night, and to do this at so many churches, as she apparently regularly did, it would have required significant organisation and the collusion of a multitude of people, all 'in on it' and conspiring together, and that this system would surely have broken down at some point in the chain? Unable to fathom how the medium had achieved it, Edwards joined a home development circle. For the first few weeks, absolutely nothing at all happened. Then things rapidly did! At their very next get-together, Edwards suddenly felt a terrible compulsion to stand up and say aloud the words that were popping into his head. He found himself saying the first word aloud, then the next, as the words flew into his mind and out of his mouth, and his voice no longer seemed to be his own. Edwards would later say, "I found I could refer to passages of the Bible that I had never read." Edwards had somehow developed the ability to go into trance, where spirits could speak through him, without him even trying! When he'd set out on his mission to prove there was no such thing as talking to the dead, little did he realize that he would end up on stage in front of sold-out audiences at huge public arenas, vividly demonstrating just how real it actually was.

When he died in 1976, he left his country house and acres of forest woodland in a Trust as The Harry Edwards Healing Sanctuary, which enabled his legacy of spiritual healing to continue. It's located in Shere in the most beautiful countryside of the Surrey Hills in South Eastern England. Having visited the sanctuary myself on many occasions, it's a perfect setting, far from the hustle of London and the surrounding suburbs. Rasmus Branch and his wife took over the running of the sanctuary after Edwards died. Branch had worked in the commercial sector in the Strand in London, far removed from the field of spiritualism, but he became great friends with reporter Maurice Barbanell, a mainstream journalist who himself became so convinced of the existence of spirits that he went on to become editor of the long-standing Psychic News. Branch writes that Harry, or 'Henry,' as he was more commonly called by those who knew him well, received 'Testimony from all over the world... bulging files of exceptional healings, from the humblest citizen to royalty, often substantiated by photographic evidence of the "before" and "after", clear for all to see... where X-Rays and biopsies proclaimed beyond all doubt that such and such a disease pathologically existed within the patient but which had somehow mysteriously vanished after help had been requested from Edwards.' Perhaps one of the most dramatic healings Edwards carried out was early on before he became well-known. It involved his young niece Vivien in the Autumn of 1952, when she was out on a tractor at the family farm. A bale of hay slipped forward from behind and knocked her off the tractor. She fell straight under the wheels. She suffered 'appalling internal injuries; her body being crushed,' Branch says. Vivien was rushed into the farmhouse and the doctor urgently called to come. When the doctor arrived, 'He was heard to say over the telephone to the hospital that she would probably be dead upon arrival.' Her eyes were described as "pools of blood." At the hospital, 'One of the doctors who examined her had actually pronounced her dead.' Henry (Harry Edwards) was quickly told about what had happened to his niece by his sister, Vivien's mother, and he immediately sent 'absent healing' to Vivien. 'At the hospital that night, the doctors fully expected her to die; but to their utter astonishment she began to make a 'remarkable recovery,' and despite their dire prognosis, within 5 weeks Vivien was fully recovered and discharged from hospital, no worse for wear than before her accident.

Harry Edwards mysterious healing powers extended far beyond just this however. According to Branch, 'Many times during his lifetime, there were numerous accounts of his having been seen and identified beyond any shadow of doubt in places where he had never been before and at times when physically he was sometimes hundreds if not thousands of miles away.' One instance involved a soldier in the Second World War called Sergeant A.F. LeRoy. He was an American paratrooper who'd broken some bones in his ankle during a parachute drop. 'The bones had not set properly and he was in immense discomfort.' A pal suggested he should write to Harry Edwards. 'The paratrooper scoffed at the idea, at first.' Then he gave in and agreed to do it. In fact, not only would he write to Edwards but afterwards he also wrote to Psychic News too, to tell them what happened as a result. The soldier explained that two weeks earlier, there'd been a farewell party for someone and he'd attended it. At the party, he'd tried to dance but his foot was too painful. Regardless, he stayed until the early hours, then took himself off to bed. 'Suddenly,' he wrote, 'I woke up and in the light from the corridor I saw a man arranged in a white overall standing by my bed with his back to me. He then seemed to put his hand right through my blankets, and gripped my leg…. He had a grip as strong as an iron wrench.' The soldier could feel his ankle and foot being physically manipulated by the man in the white coat and, 'As he did this, the pain shot up my leg.' Then, he felt his leg being placed back down on the bed, and the man in the white coat 'turned to me and smiled as if to say, "OK." When he looked at me, his face seemed to glow with a light much whiter than anything I have ever seen.' The soldier says he had never seen a photograph of Harry Edwards, nor had he even heard of him before his friend suggested he write a letter to him. When the soldier was later shown a photo of Edwards, he recognized him instantly. Branch is quick to point out however that this letter was just one of the multiple similar accounts Edwards would receive. Year upon year, the Sanctuary would get letters from people who had received distance healing from Edwards, giving accounts of 'how they have seen "a man in a white coat" in their home where either they themselves have been lying ill or a sick relative.' On one occasion, a 6-year-old child visiting the Sanctuary 'matter of factly declared, "That's the man who stands by my bed sometimes!" Surrey Live Newspaper archives describe an article written in the Surrey Advertiser in 1976 in which Harry Edwards admitted that he originally wanted to prove this spiritual healing was all a fraud, and they provide more details about how Edwards discovered his 'unusual powers.' It happened during the first World War when he was serving in the army and stationed in Persia. Edwards told the reporter that he was in charge of a gang of labourers building a railway line. 'It was a hard life,' yet, 'with only bandages and ointment he found terrible injuries healed quickly under his care.' However, 'He was unconvinced of his special power and after the War set up a print business.' Then, 'He set out to prove that Spiritualist feats can be accomplished by sleight of hand, but was dubbed a healer by mediums involved in the movement.'

Edwards 'is said to have performed his first "miracle cure" in 1935 when a patient dying of tuberculosis in Brompton hospital made a remarkable recovery with his help.' Mr Edwards, says Surrey Live, 'told of several cases where he had helped people who were apparently dying… the wife of a man with cancer of the liver went to his shop to seek aid. Within a month the man was cured.' It all began when a lady walked into his print shop in Balham. Edwards could tell immediately from her demeanour that there was something greatly upsetting

Proof of the Afterlife

her. As they got into a conversation, the lady told Edwards she had no idea why, but she had felt compelled to come into his shop. Edwards encouraged her to tell him what the matter was, and she explained that her husband had been sent home from St Thomas Hospital in London with terminal cancer and the Doctors could do nothing more for him. On this particular day, she said, she had felt so distressed at home that she had come out for a walk along the High Street. When she saw Edward's shop, she'd felt she must come inside, even though she did not know why. On hearing all this, Edwards began to tell her about spiritual healing, to which the lady, Mrs. Newland, insisted that her husband would not stand for anything like that. He was an agnostic, she said, and Edwards could not come to their home. Edwards replied that he would carry out some distance healing instead then, and Mrs. Newland left. Two days later she returned, her face beaming with joy. She quickly explained that her husband was no longer lying desperately ill in bed, but instead, he had got out of bed and made her a cup of tea! He no longer seemed to be in any pain, she said. Not long after this, her husband returned to the hospital to ask his doctor to sign him off sick from work. His doctor was not there that day however and so instead he saw a different doctor, who sent for his medical records. When the doctor read Mr. Newland's notes and reviewed his x-rays, he couldn't believe what he was reading – for the patient sitting in front of him did not look gravely ill to him at all. Rather than signing him off as "Unfit for work," the doctor signed him "Fit for work." Mr. Newland went on to live for many years after this, in perfect health. In fact, 18 years later he was invited to Harry Edwards' 60th birthday party!

In his lifetime, Harry Edwards also studied other mediums, particularly the Welsh physical medium Jack Webber. 'In 1939,' Edwards writes, 'over 4,000 persons witnessed the phenomena, from small home circles to mass seances of five hundred people.' So here is an example of the good old days when there were mass gatherings. Webber was someone Edwards had watched many times, and because the physical phenomena he was capable of producing was so dramatic, Edwards had wanted to record it for posterity, so he wrote a book detailing it all. Webber was born in 1907 in Loughor, South Wales. He was a simple man, working down the mines, and he sadly died at the relatively young age of 33 after a very short illness, not long after Edward's book became available for purchase, but it's a fantastic record of an array of the unusual physical phenomena that regularly occured during Webber's seances. Edwards brought along photographers from national newspapers with him, and there are many photographs in the book. Webber himself said he was the most photographed medium in his day. 'The photographers,' Edwards writes, 'have been official press photographers representing national newspapers who have provided their own cameras and plates and undertaken all process work in their own studios.' Some of the sitters also included, 'Official representatives of the British Broadcasting Corporation, clergymen, doctors, scientists.' Edwards' own conclusion about Webber was, 'A sceptical mind has to face the fact that the photographs and reports are true,' otherwise, 'there must have been gigantic conspiracy embracing many hundreds of people, including organisations and newspapers of note, all actively participating in fraudulent acts to deceive the public.'

Jack Webber's career as a medium might have been astonishing, but his childhood in Wales had been nothing out of the ordinary. At the age of 14, he'd gone down the mines to work. In his twenties, he would return from the mines at night and sit for mediumship. According to Edwards, his mother, Mrs. Webber, belonged to a staunch spiritualist family, and they were holding a home circle for the development of their clairvoyance. Webber's own opinion of spiritualism at the time was that it was a load of "bunk." However, his fiancé was a regular participant in the home circle, and apparently Webber wanted to keep her happy, so he went along, despite being 'thoroughly bored with the whole procedure!' During these evenings, he would end up 'invariably going to sleep.' Unfortunately for Webber however, 'Very strong healing forces soon became evident.'

As Webber unwittingly began to develop clairvoyantly, he was still extremely sceptical about the so-called supernatural powers coming through him. Edwards says it was only after visiting other home circles in the district, where the same things were happening and were being testified to by independent witnesses, that Webber began to accept what seemed to be inevitable. He was not happy about it however; because in his house at night, alone, 'loud knocks would be heard, clothes would be pulled off the bed… voices would be heard, and often Mr. Webber would forcefully express himself, telling the controls (the spirits) to leave him alone! Until quite recently,' writes Edwards, 'Mr. Webber was afraid of the phenomena'. As Webber's clairvoyant abilities in the home circle continued to grow, soon things would be physically seen, as 'heads, and hands materialized.' In April 1939, the Balham Psychical Research Society, headed by Edwards, arranged for a séance with Webber to be recorded at the studios of the Decca Record Company in London. In the recorded audio, it's possible to hear a loud baritone voice, which is said to be coming from Webber's spirit control Reuben, who claimed he was a South American teacher when he was alive. As for the obvious possibility that this had been achieved fraudulently, Edwards says, 'If the medium could produce this singing voice normally, he could obtain a good living on the concert platform without endangering his life and health at public séances.'

In other words, Webber could have simply become a singer and performed on stage to paying audiences, instead of going through the whole rigmarole of setting up seances and the charade of pretending to be the greatest medium alive. Reuben's voice wasn't coming from Webber's mouth; it was coming through a trumpet – a cone shaped object made from light-weight material, with a small hole at one end and a large hole at the other; an instrument traditionally used in seances. For some reason, it provides a source for spirit voices to speak through, or they can move it around the room, to signal their presence. Reuben's voice came independently through the trumpet; not through Webber himself. Edwards writes, 'Reuben has sung continuously for an hour without cessation, with such vigour that any human throat would have become exhausted and hoarse. The direct voice is of full loud-speaker strength, possessing a quality of tone that is distinctive, and which the medium is incapable of reproducing.' It wasn't Webber doing ventriloquism or any other kind of clever trick. There were of course accusations of fraud aimed at Webber. Julien Proskauer was President of the Society of American Magicians, and a friend of Harry Houdini, who himself became well-known for debunking fraudulent mediums. In 1946, Proskauer wrote the book The Dead do not Speak, and in it he claimed that Webber would use a telescopic reaching rod attached to a séance trumpet in order to make the trumpet appear to be levitating and moving around the room. Close inspection of some of the photographs taken during the seances were said to reveal Webber holding a telescopic reaching rod attached to the trumpet. Webber would cover the rod with crepe paper, Proskauer alleged, to make it look like ectoplasm. Perhaps this is the answer, although on the other hand, looking at just one of the photographs taken of Webber in a seance, (some of which are available on the internet, or in Edward's book The mediumship of Jack Webber), 'ectoplasm' can be seen coming from Webber's mouth and also attached to the end of a levitating trumpet, which perhaps could be the alleged telescopic rod; but there also appears to be 'ectoplasm' coming from below his naval area, while both of his hands are clearly seen strapped to the chair by ropes. How can he be using a rod coming out of his lower stomach? How can his stomach be guiding and manoeuvring the rod to wildly fly around the room?

Edwards says that early on in Webber's career, 'It was suggested that Mr. Webber should sit in a cabinet, but to Mr. Webber's normal mind, to sit in an enclosed cabinet was sufficient to induce a certain amount of suspicion.' So, Webber never did, he always sat in the circle with everyone else. Vincent Gaddis, an American news reporter and author on paranormal topics, who invented the phrase The Bermuda Triangle, wrote about Webber in Borderland Sciences Journal. Gaddis said that in January

Proof of the Afterlife

1941, in the middle of a Webber séance, 'A flash was observed emerging from a levitated trumpet,' which then fell to the ground. The lights were turned on, and 'the medium was found unconscious and bleeding from the nose and finger-nails.' Many phases of the physical phenomena produced by Webber's seances were photographed for the first time in infra-red. Edwards includes many of these photographs in his book, and there's a series of pictures which show Webber's deliberately sewn-up coat being removed from his body while his arms are tightly bound to his chair. Edwards describes how Webber's astral body can be seen in an 'exteriorized state in the process of dematerialisation'. Webber's astral head is captured in the photos, exterior to Webber's physical head. In Gaddis' opinion at least, 'Faking was out of the question,' and he says the photos have 'thrown light on the mechanism used by spirit operators... the photos reveal the spirit "voice boxes" attached to ectoplasmic cables,' and 'gripper tentacles for moving physical objects.' Gaddis said there were 'ectoplasmic tentacles of a hollow tubular nature with sucker-like ends and finger-like grippers.' Sometimes Webber would be physically moved during the séances. Gaddis reports, 'On several occasions, Webber was transported in trance from the chair where he was tightly bound to the shoulders of one of the sitters in the circle,' and he adds that 'absence of weight would be noted.' In other words, Webber would be physically lighter – otherwise, of course, he would have crushed the person whose shoulder's he was sitting on! 'He would then be returned,' or, there would be 'the complete de-materialisation of the medium's head, hands and arms.' When Webber's coat was checked, 'empty coat sleeves could be felt… then the missing parts of his body would again materialize in a flash.'

Journalist Bernard Gray, a former political reporter from Wembley Park, also wrote about a Webber seance that he attended in Balham in 1939 for the newspaper The Sunday Pictorial. For the newspaper article, Gray provided a witness testimony signed in front of a solicitor. Gray said he wanted to see proof in the form of 'physical phenomena;' but not second or third hand accounts of such things. He wanted to see it himself in person. 'I want final and complete conviction,' he writes, and says he is presenting, 'material facts which a materially minded man like me can grasp.' On the evening of the séance there were fourteen people present 'in a plainly furnished room.' Gray personally tied Jack Webber to the chair by hand and foot with double sailor knots, and for good measure he tied lengths of household cotton from the ropes to the chair legs, to ensure 'he couldn't wriggle out and back without my knowing it.' Then, 'I sewed up the front of his jacket with stout thread.' The other participants in the séance included a Metropolitan

Proof of the Afterlife

policeman, a plumber, a postman, an engineer, and Harry Edwards, the medium and healer, who was a printer by trade. All the guests took hold of each other's hands, and then the light was turned out. A red bulb remained on in the room, to provide visibility. 'Things began to happen immediately, which I personally can only compare with the miracles of the New Testament,' writes Gray, rather dramatically, but he adds that he was on high alert 'for any signs of deception.' The phenomena Gray was presented with that evening included 'the appearance, in mid-air so to speak, of a perfect human face.' Gray explains that he was sitting close enough to touch the medium, who was breathing heavily, gulping, moaning at times, then 'suddenly, he gurgles alarmingly,' after which, the face appeared in the room. 'There's the nose, and yes, the mouth. The eyes, and my God! The eyelids are moving!' Gray is mesmerized. 'The eyes, soft and natural, are looking directly into mine. I jerk myself back… it's not white and unearthly… but rather it is a human face – but softer, finer, and somehow different…' From the mouth comes a voice; "My boy, my boy, I cannot stay. I just want you all to see me…God Bless you, my boy." Then the face slowly de-materializes. Suddenly, a deep resonant voice is heard. This is Webber's Indian Spirit guide, says Gray, who tells Gray to swop places with the person next to him and to hold onto the medium's hand. The spirit voice asks if Gray can feel the material of Webber's coat. Gray replies aloud that he can, to which the spirit says, "I am dematerialising his coat and taking it off." Gray says, 'Now the coat is rubbing the other side of my wrist. Something drops to the floor, with a light, rustling impact.' "Lights on!" shouts the spirit voice. Quickly, the light is turned on, and, 'the medium is in his shirt-sleeves. He is no longer wearing his coat. Round his arms, over his shirt now, are the ropes, still fastened by my patent knots.' The strings of cotton, from the ropes to the chair are unbroken. On the floor lies Webber's coat. The spirit voice says he has done this, "To prove to you that the spirit world exists." About half an hour later, the spirit puts Webber's coat back on him, again without breaking any of the ropes or cotton threads binding Webber to the chair, and with Webber still holding the hands of Gray and the guest on the other side of him all the time. The cotton threads are all still intact. Gray writes, 'The bands and the cotton are OVER the coat.' The woman guest sitting on the other side of the medium tells Gray, "I felt the coat go through my wrist." Shortly after this, as guests swop seating places and settle down again, Gray suddenly exclaims, "I can feel something on my head!" He tightens his grip on the hands of the guests on either side of him - he wants to make sure it isn't one of their hands on his head. 'Something was pulling my hair pretty hard. I realized then with a shock that "something" was definitely fingers, yet rather different from human fingers... they felt sharper, more like claws,' and they 'seemed almost metallic at the tips.' While this sounds like some kind of weird sci-fi movie, of course having experienced the feel of claw-like fingers or finger-nails or a surgical instrument gripping and scrapping me during my "spirit operation" at the healer's house, as I described earlier in the book, this seems entirely possible to me! Gray then felt his head being pulled in the direction of Harry Edwards, who was sitting next to him now, 'til my head was touching his.' "We're being tied together," says Edwards, laughing. 'We couldn't separate,' says Gray. His hair was knotted together with Edwards' hair and they had to turn on the main lights in the room in order to unknot their bound heads!

In fact, this wasn't the only time spirits played jokes on the guests. At one of the seances, a man's spectacles were removed too. After Gray and Edwards managed to free their heads, the luminous trumpets began flying around the room at break-neck speed, and Gray spoke up, saying to the group, "I should like to be absolutely sure nobody is holding them." At this, one of the trumpets shot straight towards his head, 'with the speed of an express train.' It pulled up just short of his head; 'I cringed expecting a knockout blow,' but the trumpet stopped just in time, and it pressed itself against Gray's face, with both ends, 'As if to prove it had nothing connected to it that could be causing its movement.' Toys flew around the room too, and a bell 'rose into the air and rang in time with the group when they sang.' A toy elephant 'frolicked up and down my leg,' and a heavy table in the corner of the room 'rose straight up into the air… It settled one leg lightly on my shoulder for a moment,' then drifted to the other corner of the room 'and landed with a distinct bang.' When a cigarette lighter was flicked on, standing in front of the guests was 'the solid form of a being with outstretched arm.'

A man called Colin Evans was also present that night, and he later described his experience to Edwards. Evans explained that before the séance began, he'd taken a good look as Webber was secured to his chair. 'I scrutinized very closely the tying of the medium's arms and ankles… I made special note of the exact angle at which two looped portions of rope crossed one another under the forearm. It would have been an utter and complete impossibility to arrange precisely the same angle of crossing of the rope there, except by using both hands to do so.' Therefore, Evans concludes, it is 'An utter impossibility for the medium himself to achieve.' As the séance progressed, Evans saw the trumpets flying around the room, which he says, 'Were at considerable distances from the medium and sometimes at such distances from one another, that no persons similarly have been manipulating both trumpets, even if free to walk about and stand on chairs or the like,' and the main lights, he says, were always instantly switched on so everyone could check. As the lights came on, the medium would be seen 'still tied up with empty hands.' At one point, 'The very instant the light was switched off, materialized hands, absolutely solid, warm, and obviously "living flesh" tapped my forehead, my shoulders and my knees.' One of the ladies present also reported 'child hands clasping hers,' while she was still holding the hands of the guests on either side of her. A spirit child 'then spoke in the direct voice,' says Evans, and, 'its name was correctly given and was accepted as an evidential materialization of this lady's "dead" little girl.' The lady guest declared that the little girl, 'was not known of as having ever existed to the medium or sitters.' In other words, the lady was a stranger to everyone else in the room – they had no knowledge she'd had a daughter who had died. More spirits arrived too; Two 'dead' friends spoke to Evans, and he writes, 'I feel satisfied that I knew them both. Their voice and intonation and manner of speech.' Their voices spoke 'within a few inches of my face,' and therefore, he says, 'could not have issued from the medium's lips without at least 6 people knowing he had left the chair.' The spirit voices spoke of medical conditions that Evans suffered from but that were 'not obvious and not public knowledge.'

At another seance, a Dr. Douglas Baker was present. We'll learn more about Baker's experiences with other mediums later too, but Dr. Baker wrote of this séance, 'The medium, tied to his chair, was levitated with the chair and brought down to earth with such force that the chair disintegrated.' At a Webber séance in Lincoln, Harry Edwards writes, 'A conversation was carried on via the trumpet in French,' and, on another occasion, 'At the Sanctuary of St. Andrew in Harringay, conversations were carried on in Swedish, Portuguese, and a recital of Latin was given. It may be emphasised that Mr. Webber was an unlettered man, he rarely read a book, in fact.' A person called 'Cassandra,' also wrote about a Webber seance. Or rather, 'Cassandra' was the pen name of a male Daily Mirror columnist, who sent his account to Harry Edwards and also wrote about it in his newspaper, The Daily Mirror, on February 28th 1939. 'Cassandra' had a reputation for writing particularly scathing accounts about spiritualism. They were full of vitriol and mockery of the mediums, and he did not hold his opinions back. The séance he attended took place in North London in a small suburban house where Webber had never been before, and it was confirmed that Webber had never met any of the guests either, of which there were twelve. Cassandra begins his account with, 'I claim I can bring as much scepticism to bear on spiritualism as any newspaper writer living, and that's a powerful load of scepticism. I haven't got an open mind on the subject - I'm a violent, prejudiced unbeliever with a limitless ability to leer at the unknown; At least, I was 'til last Saturday. And then I got a swift, sharp, ugly jolt that shook most of my pet sneers right out of their sockets...' Cassandra had brought along with him the Newspaper cameraman, and they stood outside the circle of seated guests so that they could observe the proceedings clearly in plain view. He describes the other guests in his usual sarcastic style by saying, 'Almost everyone a genuine customer for a lovely phony gold brick.' Webber was strapped into his chair, and 'the lights went out and we sailed rapidly into the unknown. The medium gurgled like water running out of a bath and we opened with a strangled prayer.' As the séance got into swing, trumpets 'hurled themselves against the ceiling, books took off from their shelves. Water was splashed about.' Cassandra points out that there had been no water in the room before the séance began, and he is forced to admit, 'At no time did the medium move from his chair.' By the end of the evening, Cassandra's very reluctant conclusion was, 'Don't ask me what it all means, but you can't tell me now that these strange and rather terrifying things don't happen... I was there. I saw them. I went to scoff. But the laugh is sliding slowly round to the other side of my face.'

Mr A. J. Case, President of the Cambridge Research Society, also provided a written report to Edwards. Case says he opted to sit right next to Webber, holding his hand at all times. His experience was just as astonishing as previous witnesses. 'One of the most baffling things was the removal and replacement of Jack Webber's coat. While holding his hand, I felt a substance almost like a cobweb on my wrist, which appeared to get more solid until it assumed the consistency of cloth. It seemed to have no weight,' and, 'During the time the coat has been off the body, the arms (of the medium) have swelled so that the ropes are pressing tightly into the flesh.' Case, along with the other guests, 'tried to move the ropes a fraction, but so tight have they been (tied) that any movement of them was not possible… to insert a coat sleeve under the rope was almost an impossibility and could only have been achieved after a very long struggle – if it were possible at all,' and he emphasises, 'There was no bunching anywhere of the coat.' He says that the coat was removed from the medium in three seconds, and placed back on him within six seconds. None of the ropes or cotton tied through the button holes had been broken.

The Dean of Trinity College was also present, and Case says that at the end of the evening, the Dean told him he was 'quite satisfied that trickery was impossible, wherever the power came from.' Case saw the face of an Indian man appear – a man Case had formerly known! 'I knew him quite well when he was up at the University… at the height of his fame as a cricketer.' A lady's face materialized too. 'The face was quite solid, without colouring but obviously alive; I encouraged it to talk while it floated there... the lips moved in an attempt to answer me, but produced strange "ticking sounds" until eventually the woman whispered, "I have no pain now; I do not suffer as I used to ... isn't it glorious?" Then a man's face appeared, 'the face a look of severity, and the eyes – what I could see of them, looked piercingly into mine.' Case says the man's face had 'pronounced facial ridges in the flesh,' and, 'the set of the jaw and mouth suggested a powerful character.' Case emphasises; 'Needless to say, there were no sitters in the room resembling either face.'

In February 1940, Webber held a séance for two editors of the newspaper The South London Press. Edwards was present again, and when the photos were developed, one of them showed 'a perfect materialized hand emerging from the solar plexus region.' Another photograph showed the medium's hands held by the two editors while the coat was removed from the body. A year earlier, a reporter for Two Worlds Magazine also attended a Webber séance. He later wrote, 'My little son spoke to me... and afterwards materialized within 5 inches of my face. My little boy asked for his mummy and spoke about a bottle. "Don't you remember? You put it in my hand when I was in my coffin?" The reporter explains, 'I knew nothing of this incident, but on questioning my wife, I found she had put a small bottle of perfume in his hand the day before his funeral.' The reporter's father also came through, and he says, 'There is no possible doubt... my father's voice was very distinctive and unmistakable. He was a man of three universities. His speech, voice, enunciation and intonation were typical,' and in stark contrast to the medium's voice, which was that of 'a working man and a provincial.' The reporter went to a second seance, where Webber's spirit control told them he would "dematerialize" the medium, and, 'Before our eyes, in good red light, we saw the heads, hands, and wrists vanish, leaving just the medium's clothes in the chair.' Photographers for the Daily Mirror attended another Webber séance with Edwards, 'to attempt to obtain a photograph of the medium roped to his chair in levitation.' Webber's spirit guide told them to turn on the light and the medium 'was seen to be in the air some distance from the floor… then the sitters saw the medium descend in slow motion, turning a complete somersault as he descended, arriving on the floor on his head!' Webber was apparently unconscious for about 20 minutes, yet rather unexpectedly he sustained no injuries to his head. Edwards describes the ectoplasm Webber would produce during the seances, calling it, 'The basis for materialization of spirit people, to enable spirit people to use it to manifest themselves.' He says, "Dr Muller," one of Webber's spirit controls, 'has given the following information about this: first the ectoplasm is produced,' then 'the controls (the spirits) mould it around the etheric body of the spirit visitor (the materialising spirit), who is able to draw from the ectoplasm that power to materialize the etheric body,' and therefore, the spirit body, 'becomes as in earthly life,' and, 'the materialized etheric form is able to speak etc.' Edwards says that these materialised spirits held conversations in foreign languages. 'Conversations have taken place in tongues other than English between a materialised head and a sitter.' Jack Webber was a working-class coal miner from Wales, who had never learnt any other languages, and he was not at all well-studied in reading or writing English. Edwards describes one of the materialized faces he saw. 'The person passed over as the result of head injuries. Bandages and blood-stains are reproduced.' In other words, he means that this spirit materialised with their face covered in blood-stained bandages, as they had been when they'd died. If the person had a physical deformity when they were alive, Edwards says, 'such as the loss of a number of fingers… these are faithfully reproduced.' The spirit will materialize with their fingers missing. In the home circle I sit in, one evening we were told by our tutors to stand up and give a reading to any person in the room, according to whatever spirit came through to communicate with us. One of the mediums in the circle, stood up and immediately proceeded to describe my cousin to me, telling me that he was showing her he had only four fingers on one hand. My cousin, who died a couple of years ago, had lost a finger in a car accident when he was younger, although the medium that evening had no knowledge of this or of any cousins I had, whether dead or alive. Another night, we were working in pairs and our task was to take two cards each from a bag and read them. Mine instructed me to try to receive messages from deceased family members of the medium I was working with. My cards asked me to specifically find out how a relative of hers had died, and to receive any information I could about 'scent.' This is done to help us develop our clairsentient skills, using our five senses of seeing, hearing, feeling, smelling and tasting. As I began, I closed my eyes and the image came into my head of a man with dark hair and a moustache, although I could not see his face clearly, but he was dressed in the 1940's style of men's suits and smoking a cigarette. The partner I was working with recognised my description as a deceased relative of hers. I then saw a man from behind walking up a grassy hill into a forest. Then I experienced the most visceral vision of a car crash. The sound of metal smashing and grinding was deafening; yet at the same time it was as though I couldn't hear it like we hear ordinarily. It's hard to explain, but it was shocking and overwhelming and incredibly vivid. When I told my partner, she confirmed that a relative of hers had died in a car crash. Perhaps we could say that's quite a common way to die and I could have just guessed it, or simply made it up, and that's true, yet for someone like me who is just setting out

Proof of the Afterlife

on mediumship development, I can't discount the sounds and images of it; they were so graphic. If I had just guessed it, I wouldn't have literally seen and heard the car crash – in fact, it was probably the most striking sensations I've had since I joined the home circle. What's somewhat reassuring is that from the first time I have attended the circle, I'm not the only one there who continually doubts what they "see" and "hear." Sometimes even the experienced platform mediums in the circle question the images and sounds and words they see and hear during our exercises; because often they are cryptic or seem to make little sense until the message is given to the person it's intended for. I always thought that mediums see and hear so easily and so clearly that they never need to question the messages coming from the spirit world; but it isn't like that at all. It's a constant game of interpretation; and it's mentally exhausting! An image might come, with no words or sounds; it may be an object, for example, like a screwdriver, or a banana! It may not even be clear enough to properly see, and from this, the medium must try to work out what they are seeing and even more so, why they are seeing it. It's almost like trying to solve a mystery every time, while at the same time questioning your own sanity and wondering if it is a product of your own imagination, then using deduction and mental reasoning, to try to make sense of the message, which we seem to be constantly doing in our exercises. It's actually extremely challenging, and if anyone has ever gone to a platform demonstration or had a psychic reading, this may help to explain why the medium is not able to give the clearest messages - because what they're seeing or hearing or sensing often isn't that clear at all - or, it's so crazy that we doubt it can be real! We also practise psychometry in our group and one night we passed around a sealed envelope and had to say what was inside of it. When I held the envelope, all I could see was a giant cartoon character bunny, frantically bouncing up and down on a kid's space hopper… I presumed it was a fairly accurate representation of my own mental state and the chaos and confusion I seem to get into when I'm doing these exercises – yet actually, when the envelope was opened, it turned out that the object inside of it was related to the Falklands War, and as my tutor explained, at the time, the army had used particular vehicles called "Hoppers." Ok, so obviously I didn't get it right – but I did get hopper! On other rarer occasions for me, the spirit messages are easier. For example, one night when we were doing psychometry again, I touched the envelope and instantly saw a roman soldier walking in front of me. When the envelope was opened there was a coin with a roman solider on it.

Another time, we had to pass around a plastic letter from the game of scrabble. As I reached out to take it from the lady sitting next to me, a blue streak of light shot out of my arm toward the scrabble piece. I thought my eyes were deceiving me - I thought maybe I'd simply moved my eyes too quickly and somehow it had caused this flash of colour, although I'd never experienced something like that before with my vision. Anyway, after we had all touched the scrabble letter, our tutor asked us to give feedback on what we'd seen or felt or sensed. I explained, feeling rather embarrassed, that I hadn't got any impressions because I'd been distracted by this flash of blue light and that I thought I was just tired and must have imagined it. My tutor said, "Probably not," and asked me what the colour blue meant to me. I said I'd always associated it with healing. He then explained that the scrabble piece had belonged to his sister, who'd lived in America. Tragically, she had died about four years earlier after suffering a serious illness. He said he and our other tutor had sent regular absent healing to her throughout her illness. Another night however, it all went disastrously wrong. We were passing a sealed envelope around again, and all I saw were giant gnomes. Then the medium sitting next to me said she could see Mickey Mouse. The person next to her saw a giant rabbit, and one this went. It seemed we were all getting crazy cartoon images and none of us were anywhere close to what was inside the envelope when it was opened. We'd all descended into giggles by this point, and couldn't stop, as is often the case in our group when we get together. Our tutor simply looked at us and inquired, "What are you lot on tonight?" I don't know what was going on that evening – the spirits were probably having fun and games with us. Although, I remember speaking with contemporary Scottish medium and psychic surgeon Chris Ratter, an absolutely lovely man, and he told me he once saw a fairy in his development circle, so perhaps the gnomes I saw were real! Sometimes, I just simply draw a blank, and anxiousness sets in; which gets progressively worse and worse and I feel so embarrassed as my face gets red and I break into a sweat and get a knot in my stomach, and I feel like the stupid one in class. One night we were working in pairs and we had to try to get any deceased family member of our partner to communicate with us. As soon as I closed my eyes, I could see a man in spirit with short curly grey hair, wearing brown corduroys and holding golf clubs. I described him to my partner, who promptly and resolutely said she didn't recognise or know anyone who looked like that. I continued to try to get any more information I could, but I was struggling so badly and nothing seemed to be happening; I wasn't really seeing or sensing anything else. In the end, my partner said it could be her father-in-law, but he was bald, adding, "Well, I suppose I can take the brown trousers too!" This was so generic that at this, we both descended into giggles, which got worse when I suggested that perhaps he'd wanted hair and so that was why he had come back with some! It was a pretty abysmal reading on my part, and we couldn't compose ourselves for quite some time, as our tutors looked on in despair. Eventually, we managed to get a grip of ourselves and I tried to link with the spirit again, who I could still see, but then the scene changed to a close-up of a scaffolding pipe! I thought, "Oh God, now what do I say!" Having been told time and time again when I doubt what I am seeing, just to simply say it, I told this to my partner, dreading her reaction and worried that we'd end up in a fit of giggles again, but to my shock she explained that they'd just had scaffolding put up around their house because they were about to have some building work done. I didn't know where she lived, or anything about her life. Then, the scene changed again, and all I could see were giant Cockatiels – the tropical parrots. I could see them right in front of my face, just like I'd seen the huge flapping fish. All I could see were these great big Cockatiels, then suddenly, an aviary full of birds. As I told my partner this, she explained that her sister-in-law had Cockatiels, and so did she and her husband; they kept them in an aviary in their garden. It seemed possible now that her father-in-law in spirit was sending these images into my mind; showing her and her husband, who also sits in our circle, that he's around and knows what's going on in their lives.

Another night, we were practising giving readings in pairs and my partner kept laughing and saying, "I can't say that!" because what she was seeing was too silly - but in the end, she eventually did. She said the spirit was showing her a bunch of bananas! It sounds banal, meaningless, stupid, and she presumed it was simply coming from her own mind. She thought she had to be going mad and just imagining them – like I think every time too. After all, why on earth would one of my deceased relatives make the effort to communicate with her, simply to show her a bunch of bananas? Well, as it turned out, that day I had been rushing around a lot and I'd driven a long distance on the motorway for an appointment, then hurried back in time to get to our group. I'd left without eating any breakfast and I'd stopped off at a motorway service station where I'd bought a bunch of bananas. I ate one banana on the way to my appointment, one on the way back, and because it had taken most of the day, I had to drive straight to our circle without going home for dinner. I ate another half a banana just as I was parking outside the house where we meet. The remaining bananas were scattered on my passenger seat as I got out of the car. When I'd bought the bananas, the man at the till had asked me, "Anything else?" and I'd laughed, held up the bunch and said, "No, just these thank you." I have no idea why I held the bunch up and shook them at him! So, while this had made no sense to my partner; to me, it kind of summed up my day! And, as my tutor explained, this was spirit showing me and telling me they had been with me on that long motorway drive - they had seen me, watched me, been with me as I'd driven all that way. This was further demonstrated to me when my partner said the word, "Screwdrivers." You see, I have screwdrivers sitting around all over the house. I've never put them back in the garage after I've used them because I like to see them; they remind me of the family members they used to belong to, and it gives me a lot of enjoyment and comfort to see them, so I made the decision to leave them out everywhere. So, you see, the word "screwdrivers" means an awful lot to me – and my family in spirit were telling me that they know this; that they're aware of this, that they're watching me, that they're with me every day. It was just one word; yet it summed up so much, and as our tutors say, it's not easy or simple for spirits to learn how to communicate with us – so why would they struggle to create complex sentences when one word, or one image can sum up so much, and provide so much evidence of their existence, just as effectively and faster, and it's easier on the medium too, who doesn't have to struggle to try to understand what the words are, especially for a beginner like me?

Another time, I was sitting with a lady I had never met before in one of our open workshops. We were speed reading, swopping seats every two or three minutes. I closed my eyes to try to get spirit to communicate with me and I could see a green car that looked like an old Morris mini traveller with brown wood panels. I told her this, and she said "No." No one in her family had ever had a car like that, she said. Nevertheless, I persevered and continued to describe what I was seeing – because my tutor was sitting listening and I couldn't just sit there doing nothing, but my anxiety was getting worse and worse now, but still, I persevered and told her it was somewhere by the coast because I could see a grass verge leading to chalk cliffs beside the sea. Again, she said she had no idea what this was about. I said, "This was where you would go for holidays as children"; but I felt so stupid - because I expected her to say "No" again. After a pause however, she said, "Oh, yes! It was my neighbour's car - we didn't have a car but we used to borrow it to go on holiday to the seaside." I could see a picture clearly, of the car and her and her parents and I knew they would stop there and have picnics. Then the scene shifted to a house and I was taken by a man I sensed was the lady's father, into a greenhouse - which I described, and the lady confirmed they'd had one when she was a child. I said her father was a keen gardener and spent a lot of time in his greenhouse, to which she replied that he grew his own species of plant. Perhaps the most astonishing reading I had in our pair work exercise was when a family member in spirit came through and gave answers to questions that I had been ruminating with a friend earlier that day while walking in the park. The topic I was discussing was not usual and I was staggered that the answers I got showed my family member had heard me talking to my friend earlier in the day, discussing the subject. The lesson I've learned in my circle is to say whatever comes into my mind now – whether its words or images, or just a sense of knowing, no matter now how crazy it may seem – because as my tutors and indeed tutors I've sat with at Spiritual Association of Great Britain in Battersea, where Sir Winston Churchill and Sir Arthur Conan Doyle were members say; it's not for me, as a beginner, to try to decipher the meaning of the messages because they are not meant for me – they're for the person I'm giving the reading to; it's about their family, their life, history, and memories, not mine. In our circle, I've been given messages that are very specific family jokes, personal only to those in my family, things that no-one could guess and that are meaningless to anyone outside my family.

In my case, I usually don't hear a message; it's usually just a couple of words or more often I see the words, or words simply pop into my mind. Sometimes it's just a knowing or I see images and scenes. My tutors will then link into what I am seeing and they're able to see much more than me and give a more detailed description. It's easy to forget, but that anything comes through at all is surely a minor miracle in itself, given that they're coming from people that are supposed to be dead? I also didn't know this, but spirits often come in a group; several relatives in the spirit world all coming at the same time, wanting to talk to their relatives. Our tutors say that for them it's like a bus full of passengers arriving, all anxious to try to communicate and be heard. This helps to explain why I often seem to get confusing messages, or see different people in my mind, in the space of a few seconds. It often seamlessly transitions.

What joining the development circle has helped me to understand is that almost every medium will struggle with explaining what they are seeing or hearing when they're giving readings - because things are not always vividly clear, or the messages make no sense; it is muddied, vague, unspecific, shadowy, obscure, or very specific but indefinable in its meaning. In fact, I remember an outburst of mine one evening in the circle when I was feeling particularly frustrated. "Why can't the spirits just tell us what they mean!" I asked in exasperation. I remember seeing a clothes line with fresh white cotton sheets hanging on it one evening when I was doing a reading in pairs. Shrugging my shoulders and apologising for giving her useless information, I told the partner I was working with, only for her to say that 'cotton fresh' is her favourite scent. I had forgotten that we'd been given cards with tasks on them – mine said I had to be given a scent by the spirits and find out how they died. The spirits were showing her that they knew what her favourite smell was, but I hadn't put two and two together. It was in this same reading that I saw and heard the car crash.

But going back now to the Jack Webber seances, and Harry Edwards describes the process by which spirit materialization took place in the séance room; 'At first a vague, shadowy form is seen, darker than the prevailing light.' This form will then become denser and will often move nearer to the red light in the room, 'for closer examination,' and he explains that the spirits do this in order to allow the sitters to see them more clearly. 'The red light is about nine foot from the floor yet the materialised people are able to rise to it and expose their heads in close proximity to the bulbs.' When a spirit leaves, 'It is seen to diminish downwards as if passing through the floor.' This happens within the space of about two seconds. Simultaneously, the medium Webber emits 'gulp-like sounds' says Edwards. On touching the hands of the spirits, he says, 'They are as a rule slightly wet, yet their temperature is warmer than the hands of the sitters.' Curiously he adds that if the spirits are Chinese, then long nails can be felt.

The nephew of Jack Webber, Denzil Fairbairn published 'the back story' of Webber in 2020. He says that Webber also had a Spirit doctor called Malodar who materialised healing oils through Webber's palms, and that Malodar would guide Webber down to the marshes where he would be led to wild herbs which he would be instructed to take home and make into healing remedies for his patients. As word of Webber's abilities spread, a local family contacted him to ask for his help in trying to locate a missing family member called Mr. Morgan. For days, search parties had already been out looking for him, but they had found no trace of him. They'd contacted Webber as a last resort, and as Webber sat with them, his spirit guide came through and told him that Mr. Morgan, an elderly gentleman, was dead. 'He had drowned and his body would be found in five days' time, at a certain spot in the marsh, near to the River Loughor.' The sitting took place on the Monday, and so on Friday, five days later, 'the body was found exactly as predicted, the gentleman having been drowned as indicated.' Desmond also describes the occasion when at one of Webber's séances, a sitter suddenly exclaimed, "Look! The medium is up in the air!" A notebook too, which had been placed inside a cabinet by one of the guests 'who hoped they might receive a message from their young daughter in spirit, was found to contain the following message, "Daddy, I am happy - Daisy." Denzil also got hold of the testimony of a Mr. Harold Brown, who had attended a séance held in Cardiff in February 1938. Mr Brown testified that a hand "grasped my arm, pulled my ear and then gently pulled my wife's hair," and before the night was over, "the medium in his chair was levitated and bumped across the ceiling!"

Proof of the Afterlife

As Webber fully immersed himself in spiritualism, he moved from Wales to London and he actually found a house that had become available to rent right next door to Harry Edwards. He began a development circle where infra-red photography could be taken, and experimented in spirit materialisation. Sadly, he died just 14 months later, when only 33. Deziel explains what happened, and it seems that Webber died from a random act of kindness. He was on a train one day when he spotted a sick soldier sleeping in one of the train carriages. Leaning over the soldier, he silently gave him some spiritual healing. Unfortunately, the soldier was suffering from highly contagious meningitis and Webber contracted the disease, leading to his untimely death.

CHAPTER SEVEN

'Perhaps the most staggering incident was when a spirit materialized in the room.'

Sir Arthur Findlay, MBE, was a Magistrate, accountant and stockbroker. He was born in 1883, and awarded a Member of the British Empire for his work with the Red Cross. In his Will, he left the stately Stanstead Hall in Essex to the Spiritualists' National Union. Today Stanstead Hall, a magnificent building that looks like it comes straight from a Harry Potter book, teaches residential courses in Mediumship, and it's become famous as the foremost home of mediumistic development. Findlay, a Justice of the Peace, began his journey into spiritualism in 1918 when he was staying in Glasgow. His wife had been sent there to recuperate from an operation, and one night while he was visiting her in the rest home, he told her that he felt like stretching his legs and getting some air, and so he went out for a walk. On his walk, he passed a Spiritualist Church and his curiosity was aroused. As he explains in his 1931 book, On the edge of the Etheric, the only thing he knew about spiritualism was that his wife had been reading a book

Proof of the Afterlife

about it, and after she finished it she had offered it to him to read, but he'd rejected it as too fantastical to engage with. That night however, as he stood outside the Spiritualist Church, he felt a compulsion to go inside and see what it was all about. Pushing open the door, he quietly took a seat and watched as a lady standing at the front on the stage gave a message to a person seated in the audience. Then she gave another message to someone else, and on this went. The messages were coming from "dead people." At the end of the service, Findlay approached the medium on the stage and began to ask her questions; his scepticism on full display. In response, Findlay found himself being invited by the medium to go the following evening to a house where he would receive "proof" of what she was saying. Later, when Findlay returned to the rest home, he told his wife about the invitation. She expressed concern and advised caution: to go with a stranger to a strange house was perhaps not the wisest of choices, she told him. Regardless, Findlay decided he would go along anyway, and so the following evening, he arrived at the address he'd been given, to discover that there was to be a séance with a Scottish medium called John Campbell Sloan. Sloan was a packer in a Glasgow warehouse by day, and a medium by night. Findlay was shown to his seat in the unfamiliar house and the séance began in darkness. Soon voices could be heard, claiming to be the relatives of other people present at the séance. They were speaking aloud for all to hear, and proving their identity, and giving their knowledge about everything going on in the lives of their loved ones there that night. Findlay quite reasonably believed there must be some sort of fraud going on, even though the voices could be heard directly in front of each sitter, not coming from the mouth of the medium Sloan. Findlay found himself thinking, "What a wonderful actor there must be among us to be able to carry on like this for hours on end!" Such were his thoughts, he says, 'When suddenly, right in front of my face a strong voice spoke to me.' The voice said, "Your father, Robert Downie Findlay." Then the voice spoke of something known only to Arthur Findlay, his father, and one other man, who was now dead. Findlay later wrote, 'I was therefore the only living person on earth with any knowledge of what the voice was talking about.' What's more, a second voice could then be heard, and it was the voice of the other man who knew about the matter; his father's dead business partner, a Mr. Kidston. They were talking about something that had happened 14 years earlier, when Kidston had turned down Findlay's father's proposal that Arthur should join the business they ran. Kidston was now telling Arthur that it had been a mistake and he regretted the decision. 'Only the three of us knew about this private affair,' writes Findlay, 'and here I was in a Glasgow artisan's house, a complete stranger to everyone, being told about something known only to me and two dead men... in the company of people I had never seen before in my life.' Findlay was so fascinated by this was that he would go on to sit with the medium Sloan nearly forty times over the next five years, during which time, 'Voices spoke even when my ear was within an inch of his mouth, which was silent. Two and three voices sometimes spoke at the same time,' and he adds, 'Occasionally, the voices were so strong that they could be heard across the street!' During these seances, many of Findlay's deceased family and friends came through, and he describes an incident where a friend and fellow researcher at the Society for Psychical Research, which Findlay had now joined, asked Findlay one day if he would take a friend of his to Sloan's house for one of the seances. Findlay agreed, and went for dinner with the researcher's friend before taking him to see Sloan. Other than knowing that he was a friend of a friend, Findlay says he knew nothing more about the man, and their conversation prior to the séance was on topics of general interest only, not personal. When they arrived at Sloan's house, the séance quickly got underway and a voice could be heard 'clearly and distinctly' addressing the man Findlay had brought along with him. The man asked the voice who they were, and the voice replied, "When on earth I was known as King Edward VII. I must thank you for all your kindness to my wife, Queen Alexandra. I do not know how she could have gone on without you."

When the séance was brought to a close, Findlay asked the man he had brought with him about his about his relation to the Queen. The man replied, "I am the controller of her household." Not long after this, having heard about the incident, Queen Alexander herself sat in a séance with Sloan too, along with Sir Arthur Conan Doyle and a number of scientists including an American man called Mr. Byrd. Mr. Byrd received a message too; 'A friend of his came back, giving his name and spoke to him, reminding him of the occasion when they were together on Brooklyn Bridge and what they then talked about,' to which Mr. Byrd replied, "That is all true, but how can you speak to me when you are dead…?" Findlay says that he was careful not to be fooled by Sloan. When he went back again after attending the first séance, he says, 'When a voice spoke, I put my ear right close to his mouth. I felt his breath, my ear and his lips were just touching, but not a sound was to be heard.' Moreover, 'two and three voices sometimes spoke at the same time.'

Sloan's first experiences of spirit happened in his youth when, 'he was often disturbed by rapping's and strange voices which he could not understand.' When he became a medium, he refused to ever take any payment. Findlay explains, 'His reward, he says, is in sending away some sorrowing one with the knowledge that life continues beyond this world.'

Proof of the Afterlife

Findlay kept records of the séances he attended with Sloan. 'I have notes of thirty-nine different seances; eighty-three separate voices have spoken to me, or to personal friends I have brought with me, and two hundred and eighty-two separate communications have been given to me or to them; voices from etheric men, women and children who have materialised their vocal organs and lungs and speak as we do, without any connection whatever with the medium, except the ectoplasmic substance necessary for materialisation.' Findlay was particularly impressed when he was accompanied by people Sloan had never met before. On one occasion, Findlay took with him a recent widow. In fact, her husband's funeral had been that very day. 'I introduced her to Sloan by another name,' Findlay points out, before he explains what happened. Immediately after the séance began, a voice could be heard in the room, independent of Sloan, saying, "Why did you give the lady's wrong name? We know who she is, and her husband, Louis Pearson, is here to speak to her." An emotional voice then spoke, 'remarking that it would take him some time to recover from seeing his earth body burned.' At another séance, Findlay brought with him a Professor from the University of Glasgow. 'A voice spoke to him in a language I did not understand. He replied in the same language and the conversation went on for some time.' When the séance finished, Findlay enquired of the professor what language was he speaking in, to which the professor replied that it was Welsh. "I am Welsh, and the voice which spoke to me gave the name of an old gardener I employed... he knew all about me and what he said was quite true." Perhaps the most staggering incident was when a spirit materialized in the room. Findlay writes, 'Nothing was more amazing than the return of Eric Saunders... not only was his evidence remarkable and everything checked later as correct, but he was seen when speaking.'

In his book Rock of Ages, Findlay says a spirit told him, "I have a body which is a duplicate of what I had on earth, the same hands, arms, legs, and feet, and they move in the same way as yours do. This etheric body I had on earth interpenetrated the physical body." The "etheric" is the "real body," said the spirit, and this is "an exact duplicate of our earth body." When we die, we emerge from the flesh of our body and continue on in the 'etheric' world. The 'etheric' body continues to function, "just as our body on earth functioned." This 'body' is "just as substantial." Spirits can touch, feel, see, and your mind goes with your etheric body, the spirit said. The world of spirit is, "a real, tangible world... everything is real to us. We can sit down together and enjoy each other's company just as you can... We have the same feelings as you have.... All is tangible but in a higher degree of beauty than anything on earth."

CHAPTER EIGHT

"How would you like to feel the hand of a man who's been dead for one hundred years?"

Stewart Alexander is one of the few current physical mediums that exist in the world; a very rare breed of mediums who can produce physical phenomena. He has now since retired, but he spent many decades giving small demonstrations around the country. As Professor David Fontana, who has been involved in psychical research for 30 years says in the introduction to Alexander's autobiography, 'There is a shortage of good first-hand accounts by physical mediums,' and it is certainly the case that much of what happens in closed circles across the country seldom gets written into publication and is lost forever, which is such a great loss. Professor Fontana attended many sittings with Stewart Alexander, at both public demonstrations and in Stewart's closed home circle, which took place at the home of member Ray Lister in Hull. Fontana describes how the séance room they used, 'has only one door... No hidden trapdoors or entrances, and no hiding places; no possibility of accomplices entering the room.' Fontana believed

Alexander to be completely genuine in all that occurred, no matter how extraordinary, and Alexander himself says, "That which I relate may often leave readers incredulous." Like most mediums, Alexander didn't set out from childhood to become a medium, and little did he know, but he would end up sitting in a cabinet and producing spectacular feats of physical phenomena. He became interested in Spiritualism, he says, after reading Sir Arthur Findlay's book On the Edge of the Etheric. In particular, Alexander was fascinated by Findlay's account of the physical medium John Campbell Sloan and the independent voices that would speak in his séance room, and he craved to know more, so he started going to the Spiritualist Church near his home with his brother. It wasn't long before he found himself being invited to join a home circle. He went along to it, but he says he was not impressed by what went on there, and so eventually he decided to set up his own circle. One night a week, for week upon week, he and his small group of fellow enthusiasts sat in the dark, waiting; but nothing happened. Then, one night as they sat around the table in silence, and with Alexander's mind turning to the cup of tea they would have when they finished, he suddenly heard a voice in his ear, telling him to turn out the light. As he did so, he says he became aware that "something", 'a presence – outside of myself, was rapidly approaching me...How does one attempt to describe that which is were turned off and a prayer was read aloud. Walter the control spirit invited a female in the audience to sit at the table. He asked her if she 'would like to see his etheric hand materialised in a physical shape?' The lady replied, "Yes please," and, 'a black matter comes out and spreads onto the table. I am sitting about three metres from the little red table and can see that the matter is developing in the palm of a hand; it becomes red and a bit transparent.' Then, 'the hand materialises and puts itself on top of the woman's hand. It is a warm and normal hand, the woman says. "Yes, indeed it is," says Walter, "as we still are very human even though our physical bodies on earth are gone." Then Walter places his hand in the middle of the table, and raps on it with his fingertips. "Yes, it is just a regular hand," the spirit says. Then his hand disappears. Strommen notes, 'We see that the hand dematerialises into the same matter as it started out with, and then it is gone.' As Walter moves around the room, Strommen can hear he is patting the hands of the woman on his left-hand side. 'He walks past me. I can feel the air pressure… something icy on my neck, and a severe thrust in my right ear!' Canadian medium Carolyn Molnar also describes her experience on her website, when a hand 'made of ectoplasm,' grew from Stewart's chest, and, 'it touched me.' There were approximately 60 people present at the spiritual retreat where it happened. Alexander was sitting 'in a square cabinet with the front curtain open and a soft indescribable? I can only say that as it forced itself to merge with my very being, every nerve and every muscle in my entire body began to react violently… uncontrollable spasms and tremors. At the same time, my consciousness seemed quickly to locate itself outside, behind and to the left of my body and from that position I observed my mouth fall open and with a rush words issued forth.' This was understandably quite a shock to Alexander as well as the rest of the group! 'To say this was unnerving, for us all, would be to understate everyone's feelings.' However, he adds that this was the only time he would ever be scared again. He was also bothered by a thought he couldn't shift; had this all just been his own, over-active imagination? He became consumed with self-doubt. He didn't want to be fooling himself, or anyone else for that matter. Well, not to compare me, a mere beginner to the likes of revered mediums such as Alexander Stewart, but we practise "blending" with spirits in our home circle, and one night in pairs I tried to link in and make contact with spirits when I suddenly saw a young Victorian workman, and my task in this exercise was to allow this spirit to take over my body, and as I silently gave the spirit permission, I could feel his body becoming mine – and I had the impression that I was now seeing through his eyes as I described to my partner and tutor that the young man was shouting to acquaintances I could see that he knew who are passing-by in the cobbled street as he sat on a wall. My shoulders felt somehow bigger, my arms and thighs too, and it was like his larger hands took over mine. Well, my tutor 'linked-in' – so that he could see what I was seeing. In the London street scene, he could describe what I was seeing, exactly as I was seeing it, but in far greater detail. Of course, readers will think I'm just making all this up. One night, our task was to meditate and bring back something given to us by spirit. I don't mean physically but clairvoyantly. We have to know what the item is and who in the circle it is intended for. It's often a very difficult exercise – but we do it every week and there's no escaping! This night, when I asked spirit for an item, they presented me with two sticks, and told me who I had to give them to. I thought to myself, "Oh no, this is so embarrassing. How can I give them two sticks?" Not only that, but the medium I was told to give them to had been a drummer in a rock band – so naturally, I assumed this had happened because I knew this information about her and my mind had come up with them, although they didn't look like drum sticks. When it was my turn, I explained what had happened and rationalised aloud that surely this was because I knew she had been a drummer. Well, our tutors push us hard and so they told me to go back into the meditation and look more closely at the sticks. As I did so, one of the tutors linked-in and saw them too, and they asked me to describe the sticks in more detail – what size, shape, colour were they, was there anything on them, what else was around them? As I looked more closely at the sticks in my mind, I began to see symbols carved into them, and suddenly, as I expanded my vision, the scene transformed into what looked like an outdoors ceremony with a big fire in the woods at night. I was given the word "Druid" by spirit, and so that's what I said. My tutor could see the symbols and described them to me – in more detail than I did; which ruled it out as all being a product of my own fevered imagination. To my utter astonishment, as I described the scene aloud, the medium who the sticks were for said, "Well, my father is a Druid high priest." This was something that none of us in the group had known. He apparently lives in another country and had been a Druid High Priest for many years. On another occasion we were meditating one night as we sat in circle, and we were led into a guided meditation by one of our tutors, then after perhaps ten minutes, we were left alone in the meditation to simply see if we got any contact from spirits. Suddenly, I began to hear and feel footsteps coming toward me. I tried to rationalise it and tell myself it had to be the music, but there were no sounds like pounding footsteps in the music. The strange thing was, even though they were coming straight toward me; big, heavy footsteps like marching boots, they never reached me. I kept thinking there must surely be an impact when they reach me – but no – they just kept pounding away but not going through me or past me. Surely it had to be my imagination? After the meditation ended, we individually gave feedback about what had happened. Before I got a chance to give mine, one of the mediums in the group said she had felt as though she was being touched, and at this, one of my tutors laughed and said, "I could feel footsteps." I realised then that I hadn't imagined it after all.

In Stewart Alexander's case, when the spirit's body entered his in that rather violent way, it thoroughly unnerved him, quite understandably, and as the days passed and he thought about what had happened, doubts began to plague him – surely, he had imagined it? So, in order to get to the bottom of it, he decided to carry out a test. He asked his wife to write down something of her choice on a piece of paper before she went out for the evening, and to seal it in an envelope without telling him what she had written. His wife duly did this, then went out, and shortly afterwards Alexander went off to his home circle. While he was there, he asked the presence he had sensed previously to tell him what his wife had written down. He didn't hear a reply, but he got an impression in his mind of a dog running up and down a river bank barking, with the sun pouring down on the scene. Later that night, when his wife returned home, he opened the sealed envelope in front of her. She'd written; 'Sun shining, dog running up and down river bank barking.' Alexander believed this had to be proof of "the presence". However, within a couple of days again, the old self-doubts began plaguing him again and he told himself that it had to have been a case of telepathy between himself and his wife. He carried on sitting in the home circle, with this uncertainty constantly in his mind, and it wasn't until he went to a séance with the medium Leslie Flint in London that his opinion changed. 'For over two hours,' he writes, 'we heard and sustained conversations with loved ones who had passed through the gates of death and returned to speak to us in their own individual voices.' Flint did not do this through ventriloquism or other tricks, although some accused him of fraud, but rather, the voices were coming from all over the room. Often the voices would be heard a breath away from a sitter's face. Leslie Flint, who died in 1994, was a very rare medium who was capable of producing spirit voices not from his own mouth but independent of him: the voices could be heard in the corners of the room, or right in front of the sitter's face. A very good friend of mine now, who has been a medium for many decades, told me about his own experiences when he was at a séance at Flint's house, many years ago. My friend was adamant when I questioned him about whether it could have been produced by trickery; he said this was impossible in his own experience, and that it had been very real; the voices, he said, were coming from all over the room and no-where near where Flint was sitting. My friend is an exceptional medium and spiritual healer, while also being the most down to earth person too and highly sceptical. He's spotted the frauds over the years and wasn't shy in describing them to me in confidence. He enjoys a good laugh too – but he doesn't suffer fools gladly and always speaks his mind. He has his feet firmly planted on the ground, and formerly worked as in a profession before retiring. It's also worth remembering that he would have been able to tell if Flint was faking it, because he would have been able to "link in" and suss it out. Besides which, each voice was different and individually unique, he said. As for Stewart Alexander's visit to see Leslie Flint, well he returned again a few months later with some members of his home circle. This time, he was even more impressed. 'I heard the voice of my grandmother; she had been a mother figure to me,' he later wrote. Alexander surely have would be able to tell if it was his own grandmother's voice; the voice of a woman he considered as close to him as a mother? So, he returned to his evenings in the home circle with renewed determination to have the same things happen in his own group, and for week after week, then month after month, until the months turned into years, they waited, and they waited, and the doubts dominated Alexander's mind; because if Leslie Flint could do it, why couldn't they? In fact, it would be 13 long years before a breakthrough came! Imagine how disheartening it must have been to have sat for so many years, without anything happening; but their determination and persistence finally paid off! On the night it happened, they'd followed the usual procedure; sitting in silence in a circle in the dark. One hour passed by, then another, and eventually the evening was called to a close and the light was turned back on. Two or three members left immediately, but Alexander and a couple of others sat chatting over a cup of tea. Suddenly, he went into trance and the voice of a spirit began to be heard out-loud, coming from inside the trumpet. The trumpet was sitting upright on a small table and it started to rise up into the air. This was what the group had been waiting for, for so long; for something physical to happen! At the time, of course, Alexander didn't know what was happening because he was in a deep trance, but after the voice went away and the trumpet stopped moving, they quickly told Alexander all about it as he was brought out of trance. From that night on, Alexander's physical mediumship began to develop until he became known as one of the very few genuine physical mediums alive today. Interestingly, he explains that the purpose of the cabinet is, in his opinion, 'not to hide from view the kind of tomfoolery and chicanery suspected by cynics, but rather to concentrate the vital energy from which the entire materialisation was made possible,' and soon, voices, hands and entire bodies would start to appear in the room. Although Alexander has retired from public demonstrations now, Warren James from the Blue Circle development group based in Coventry, says he attended one of his séances at Cober Hill Conference Centre near Scarborough. He writes, 'For over 20 years Stewart Alexander has given thousands of seekers the greatest experience and gift that one could ask for during this modern day – he has given people assurance that their deceased loved ones are only a thought away, and that it is possible to link the two worlds together.' The séance took place in 'bright red light.' One of Alexander's spirit helpers "Freda Johnson" gave a message that she had a spirit with her called "Derek", who had died four years earlier. A lady among the guests called Violet spoke up and said she believed this message could be for her. Freda then gave the word, 'Goodison,' to which Violet said that Derek's ashes had been scattered at Goodison Park Football Club! Then, Freda said Violet's sister had instructed her to say 'just one word that she hoped would mean a great deal to her.' The word was "Duck," to which Violet laughed out loud and 'acknowledged that she had once tried to rescue a duck whose head was stuck.' Nick Shutler attended a York séance and he also wrote about what happened; 'Stewart's arm was lifted from the chair, the nylon cable tie passing right through the medium's arm yet staying securely tied around the wooden chair!' Walter Stinson, the nephew of the medium Mina Crandon and one of Alexander's control spirits could then be heard. The spirit 'Walter' was heard asking one of the guests, a lady called Karen sitting closest to the medium, to verify what had just happened. "Would you feel the arm of the chair? Is the strap still there?" "Still there," Karen replies, and "Still intact." The spirit Walter asks her if she has let go of Stewart's hand at any moment. "No, I still have hold of Stewart's hand!" "Then," says the spirit, "I hope you will agree that you have witnessed the passing of living matter through living matter, umm?" He asks one of the other guests to turn on the light so that everyone can see. Shutler writes, 'We could all clearly see the intact cable tie.' Walter says, "I hope that it demonstrates quite clearly how close our world is to yours," and he adds, "We take every opportunity that we can in order to confirm that we are who we claim to be! That we are living on in the world beyond your own! How we can manipulate physical matter itself." Shutler says another spirit arrived next, called "Freda," a regular visitor who often comes through during Alexander's seances. She explains 'the difficulties involved for people spirit-side who are inexperienced at speaking through an entranced medium.' After this, a Scottish man in the audience is invited to sit in front of the medium. Suddenly, a spirit voice can be heard, "Jim, we're still the same over here." It's the voice of his father. "Nothing changes. We're still the same people we always were. How are you? I am delighted to see you, we're here together, we are all here together. I will never forget you," he tells his son, "I think of you every day." The control spirit Walter then returns and asks another of the ladies in the group called Hazel, to come up and sit next to the medium. "Hazel, watch closely," he tells her. "Tell the folks what you can observe?" A few moments pass by and Hazel says, "Yes, yes, I can see a hand on the far edge of the table and one of the fingers is extended." A couple of moments go by and she says, "The hand is now moving towards the middle of the table and the thumb has now moved out and all the fingers are extended. He has now crossed the whole of the table." Witnessing this, Shutler writes, 'I can also see this from my position in the séance room.' Hazel continues to explain what is happening, "Yes, it is definitely quite a large hand. It's drawing back now a little. That is amazing!" Walter asks Hazel, "How would you like to feel the hand of a man who's been dead for one hundred years?" Then he instructs her to place her right hand upon the table with her palm placed downwards. At this point, they bring Alexander out of trance so that he can see it too. Shutler writes, 'The ectoplasm hasn't actually taken shape yet, it is sort of pulsating.' Then, "It is taking shape!" Alexander says, "And there is a hand coming out of it." At this point, Alexander appears to be in some discomfort 'as the ectoplasm pulls hard on his solar plexus.' Then, 'The hand grasps Hazel's hand, and Hazel exclaims that she can feel her hand being held. "It is a human hand, yes," she says. "It's very, very warm and he's shaking." At the same time, Alexander says, "Oh my stomach. It's a very strong hand. Its gripping mine now. Oh, that is wonderful! He's letting go now…" Another person who writes about attending an Alexander séance is Kai Mugge, who was present in April 2008. Mugge described himself at the time as a '39-year-old social-pedagogue and film-maker by profession, who studies the history of spiritualism, now more than 20 years.' Mugee begins his account with, 'Every sitter is thoroughly searched at the entrance of the room.' Then, as it begins, 'We can observe the medium introducing his trance-state through jerking, breathing and several abnormal face-expressions.' The lights are turned out, leaving the room in darkness. An opening prayer is said, followed by some music 'until the first control addresses the sitters with a warm welcome.' The spirit is "White Feather", one of Alexander's controls who acts as a gatekeeper to all the spirits trying to come through. Then, "Christopher" comes through. He's another regular visitor at the seances and a spirit child. The medium's voice has now become a 'fast speaking, childish voice, frequently laughing at his own jokes.' Alexander is sitting in front of the cabinet, next to a small illuminated table. Walter arrives and requests the red light to be switched on in order to show the plastic binds strapping the medium to the chair. Walter then asks a lady who is sitting next to Alexander to place her hand on top of his left hand. 'Immediately an indefinable short noise is heard, and the sitter announces that the arm has simply rushed into the air.' The control spirit asks for the red light to be turned on again and, 'Everybody can see Mr. Alexander, his right arm at head-height, while on the arm–rest the two cable-binds hang unopened.' In other words, the medium's hand has risen up into the air even though everyone can see that the cable tie around his wrist is still secured – it should not be possible for Alexander's hand to move. The female guest is requested by the spirit to check the ties and, she 'confirms that the cable ties are still connected with the arm-rest.' The red light is switched off again at the request of Walter, and, 'Again, an immediate noise is heard, and now the sitter confirms that the arm is back on the arm-rest, bound like before, all happening within a second or two.' Hazel checks the bindings again and they remain unbroken. There's a faint noise, and 'the direct voice of Dr. Barnett,' can be heard now, who explains 'he now only speaks through the ectoplasmically formed voice-box, to hold back enough energy to become materialised later in full form.' Walter then tells the group he is going to materialise his hand upon the illuminated table. Mugee says, 'I can clearly see the table's surface.' At first, 'A black mass seems to swell, gradually morphing into the middle of the table's surface.' The spirit invites everyone in the room to come closer to the table to observe more clearly. 'The mass now is reducing to a size of a very big hand...but still with no features.' Then, 'the mass seems to reorganise, and I can clearly see something like a claw or malformed, very big hand.' Then the hand changes again. 'A clumsy hand now becomes more and more visible, now beginning slowly to behave like a human hand.' It is 'moving fingers,' and it turns from one side to the other. 'The hand grabs the much smaller woman's hand.' She tells the group, "It is a dry, warm and seemingly a male hand." The hand shakes hers, then disappears. Everyone can see Alexander is still seated and tied by both arms to his chair, but Walter announces that he wants to ensure no-one in the room can be left in any doubt that the hand which appeared was not the hand of the medium, and he asks for Alexander to be freed from the cable ties. Then he asks everyone in the room to place their hands on the table, including Alexander. The red light is still on and 'within a few seconds, from the side of the medium, suddenly a ninth hand appears above the lit section.' It is a 'big, dry and male hand,' that 'touches and manipulates the hands of all sitting round the table.'

There's another account of an Alexander seance provided by Tom and Lisa Butler who run the website atransc.org, investigating electronic spirit contact. They wrote about what happened when they went to the home of Alexander's circle leader Ray Lister, in Hull. Alexander was strapped to his chair with cable ties, and he sat in a cabinet with a cloth frame. Luminous tabs were stuck to his knees and on the curtain, so that any movement of either could be observed. The sitters on either side of Alexander held his hands throughout. A round table was positioned in front of him. An opening prayer was said by the circle leader Ray Lister, then music was played as Alexander went into trance. 'It was only a few minutes before we heard the first voice,' wrote the Butlers. It was Alexander's primary spirit control, "White Feather." Walter Stinson's voice could then be heard too, telling the room 'that he had discovered after death, he lived in a very real world.' A world, 'that in many ways was very physical.' "Your world to you is a world of reality, but I tell you that your world is temporary. Our world is the world of ultimate reality." He said, his world, 'was very similar to ours, that it was a very substantial world; a world of fellowship and infinite beauty.' A spirit hand materialised at this seance too. 'A blob of ectoplasm could be seen on the illuminated table top. It slowly formed into a large hand which Walter said was his. It knocked on the table.' Then, 'The hand moved toward Brian's hand, and Brian announced that it was holding his hand and that it felt like a human hand.' Everyone was invited to place their hands on the table, and Alexander's hands could be clearly seen. Then, 'The dark shape of a large hand suddenly came,' and the hand knocked on the table for all to see.

A man called Christopher Charles Howarth also attended an Alexander séance. In Howarth's book The Vision the Voice, he says he himself always thought he could hear a voice in his head, talking to him. His curiosity to find out what the voice was led him to Harrogate Spiritualist Church, and he would go on to become a member of a spiritualist investigative group called The Noah's Ark Society. At the group's seminar in Hove in 1994, with about 50 attendees, Howarth says he witnessed one of Alexander's demonstrations. 'It was all done in good light', he says, with an opening prayer, then Alexander went into trance. Howarth says he heard his name being called and he was asked to come up to the front where Alexander was sitting. A spirit voice said to him, "Please pick up the pliers." Howarth thought, "Oh no, not me! They all looked at me." The spirit must have read his mind because the next thing they all heard was, "Do not worry, just grab his skin in a lump with the pliers, he cannot feel anything!" So, Howarth did it, taking the pliers and squeezing Alexander's skin with them! 'There was a big bruise appearing on his forearm, but everybody was smiling. I could not understand it.' In shock, Howarth returned to his seat. The following morning at breakfast, Alexander asked to talk to him. He said he understood that it was Howarth who had squeezed the skin of his wrist in a tight grip with the pliers during the séance, and he proceeded to show Howarth his wrist. Inexplicably, there were no bruises, no marks of any kind. "They look after me you know," Alexander told him. Lew Sutton, writing in the December 2011 edition of Psychic News also reported on an Alexander séance that took place in 2011 at Cober Hill Conference Centre with 90 people in attendance. 'Alexander's seances have been described many times before in the Psychic Press…There is always verbal evidence from loved ones, as well as the paranormal manipulation of matter… Voices are heard via direct voice.' Evidence is given to a man present called Freddie Giddings. "My grandmother came," Giddings told Sutton afterwards. "She asked if I remembered the green wine." Giddings then explains the relevance of this. "When I was a small boy, I used to visit her and she always gave me a small glass of Crabbies Green ginger wine," and he emphasises, "Not just occasionally, but every time I went." It was something he said he hadn't thought about for many years.

Another man called Douglas Glasby gave his account of an Alexander séance in 1996 in a google chat group. Through further research I discovered that Glasby used to write for the Noah's Ark Society Newsletter. The seance was held at the home of Ray Lister, and Glasby's wife accompanied him there. As usual, the séance was opened with a prayer, followed by some music. White Feather's voice came through first, 'quickly followed by Christopher,' the lively spirit child, 'who soon had the sitters in near hysterics.' Then, luminous trumpets began dancing around the room, going all over the place, 'swinging to the music and occasionally rapping upon the ceiling.' One of the trumpets came toward Glasby. It 'homed in' upon his head, 'and after tapping it a couple of times, it gently stroked my cheek.' Then, 'it hovered in front of my face and I could hear a voice, no more than a whisper.' Glasby says that because he is partially deaf, he was only able to make out a few words, 'but I was assured by nearby sitters that my late wife Joan was speaking.' Just before the voice faded away, 'All sitters, myself included, heard a resounding kiss from the trumpet.' At a later point, the trumpets danced again, and one came toward Glasby again. 'Through it I heard the name James Hudson.' This was 'wonderful evidence' for Glasby because Hudson was a close friend who had died. 'James Hudson was a Spiritualist researcher friend of mine.' Even more evidence was to follow; 'Through the trumpet, still in position in front of my face, I heard a slightly stronger male voice.' The voice uttered the words "Changi", and, "We sweat blood," along with the name "George Clarke," and 'other words relating to South East Asia.' Glasby did not understand what the message meant, but he had been a prisoner of the Japanese in Changi during World War II, fifty years earlier. However, he says, 'My mind was left in utter turmoil… George Clarke, where did he fit in? There were huge gaps in my memory and I could not place the man, and yet by his words I knew that he knew me at that time.' His confusion continued through the evening, and the following morning he was still none the wiser. 'I feverishly searched through my Japanese memorabilia,' he says, trying to work out who this George Clarke was, but he found no clues. Then, he remembered he'd also stored some of his war-time collection in a small cupboard, so he went to the cupboard and searched through that too. Inside, he found a small carboard box which contained old Christmas cards. He looked inside, 'And there amongst them I discovered a folded card.' The front of the card had a palm tree on it, 'and over the palm were the words "P.O.W. Changi Camp 1944." Inside the card someone had written the word, 'MENU,' and below this they'd written a choice of dishes, designed, says Glasby, 'by seven young men thrown together in adversity,' including Glasby himself. The prisoners of War had managed to scavenge assorted bits of food from around the prison camp. Below the menu were the words, "Coffee and Cigars," with exclamation marks; 'All wishful thinking,' says Glasby, 'in the most dire of circumstances. We at the time suspected that no P.O. W. would be allowed to survive.' Together, the seven men had decided, 'To hell with it: we would have a final get-together.' Looking at that card, it all came back to him. Glasby turned the card over, and found the seven men's names written down. 'Half-way down on the left-hand side was the name Gunner George Clarke.... My search was over.'

Jostein Strommen, from Baslet Psi Association in Basel, Switzerland, describes his experience of attending an Alexander seances in April 2008. He explains that the séance room was about 50 metres square in size, with the cabinet on one side of the room. The cabinet was about one square metre, and inside was a chair with arms. In front of the cabinet was a small table with red fabric covering it. On the table were two trumpets and some electro strips. Before the séance began, Strommen says, 'I now thought I would take the opportunity, whilst being alone in the room, to check out the chair, the table, the cabinet, and the equipment.' He discovered that the cabinet was a very simple construction, 'A cloth that was attached to some poles that formed a square.' The curtain was open facing the audience. The electro strips on the table were of a type that could be purchased in a hardware store. 'When you pull them out, you can hear a clicking sound, and when you have put them in place, they cannot be pulled apart. They have to be cut off.' Outside the cabinet, the floor was wooden and the sitters' chairs had been arranged upon it in rows with the cabinet in the middle of the rows. The windows were covered with black plastic. 'Nothing seemed strange,' he says. Strommen sat in the first row with a good view. The lights red light lit from below.' At one point, 'A concentrated, thick fog appeared to leak from Stewart's solar plexus area.' It 'slowly coalesced into a mass, then evolved into a hand with webbed fingers and finally into a fully male hand, right before my eyes! I heard gasps of surprise from those sitting nearby.' She heard a voice say, "Keep still", and then the hand 'moved across the lit table and gently tapped the top of my hand. The hand was large and well-defined.' The skin felt 'warm – warmer than my own.' Another witness was Bradley Harris, who also went onto to become a medium himself. He wrote in his own book of how on numerous occasions with Stewart Alexander he witnessed 'forms slowly dematerialising by melting into the floor,' and of seeing 'a white piece of ectoplasm on the floor, just outside the cabinet, rise up to form a head shape, which in a matter of seconds rose in a fountain of ectoplasm to form a fully materialised spirit form.' Bradley remarks that seeing the dematerialisation of a spirit who is a loved one could be distressing to any family members present. 'When a loved one that they have been embracing would start to dematerialise outside the cabinet' sometimes, 'a spirit would hold onto the loved one's hands, not wanting to go, but being unable to hold the power.' Then, 'They would melt into the floor.'

Alf Winchester wrote in Psychic News in 2003 of his experience. In the séance room was a specially constructed table, 'which had a glass top that was under-lit with a red light. From the direction of the medium, a lump of ectoplasmic matter was seen to move onto the table.' Then the hand appeared, 'almost like someone placing a hand in a glove; a large right hand with quite thick fingers was seen to emerge from the matter.' The fingers began to move, 'before retracing back into the lump of the matter.' After this, Walter asked for the table to be taken away and for the curtains of the cabinet to be closed with Alexander inside of the cabinet. Alexander was out of trance at this point, and he said he could see a light inside the cabinet. 'The curtains parted and a faint orb of diffused light was seen to dart from the cabinet and return.' This happened several times, and the light increased in intensity, then Walter 'in materialised form, left the cabinet carrying the orb in his right hand,' and he walked around the room, 'showing it to the sitters.' Walter then returned to the cabinet and announced that a visitor was here, who was known to a number of the sitters present, and 'that he was going to attempt to materialise.' The curtains of the cabinet 'flew open and a person's footsteps could be heard walking from the cabinet, saying excitedly, "It's Alan, it's Alan," in the unmistakable tones and mannerisms of Alan Crossley.' Alan was someone Alf had known knew very well through their spiritual research together. Alan then 'went around the circle and enthusiastically approached and greeted only those persons whom he knew.' Alan came to Alf, 'talking exuberantly in a frail sounding but still loud voice,' and then, 'grabbed my head and shook it wildly, and then took my hands and vigorously shook them.' Alan told the group that he himself had sat in many materialisation circles, when he was alive, 'but he never thought that he would have the opportunity to be the one who materialized, and was amazed and delighted!' He told them that he'd watched the other materialised forms come out of the cabinet from behind the curtains too, which parted in the middle. Alan said he'd been able to 'closely observe three materialised forms within the circle at exactly the same time,' and, 'they could be clearly seen in good red light.' Alan said he also watched a dematerialisation. He 'observed how the facial features had begun to crimple as if melting like wax before a flame.' He told them the materialised spirit's face 'had begun to fall in upon itself and his very figure began to sink downwards.' Alf says that when the figure disappeared, it left behind 'a mound of snow-white pulsating energy on the floor immediately in front of the cabinet curtain.'

CHAPTER NINE

"There he stood. Hair - spiky as always. Eyes - so, so blue."

When Alan Crossley was alive, he was an avid attendee of seances, and in particular, he became heavily involved in the Leicester home circle of the medium Rita Goold. 'Materialised Figures Appear at Home Circle,' wrote Psychic News in February 1983. 'SOLID spirit forms, an experienced Spiritualist told PN last week, are being obtained at Rita Goold's Leicester home Circle. Spiritualist Alan Crossley testified that one figure appeared in "a beautiful lace dress." Another manifested in "a complete military uniform." He also said he was reunited with his wife. "My wife Irene, who passed four years ago, manifested to me on no less than four occasions with individual mannerisms and characteristics so familiar to me." More rather remarkable physical experiences apparently happened with the medium Rita Goold too, involving a little spirit boy called Russell. The story of Russell begins one evening at the home of Gwen and Alf Winchester, in Essex. They had lost their son Russell when he was just a child. One evening, Gwen, a trained soprano, had left Alf home alone to go out singing. As Alf settled in

Proof of the Afterlife

for a quite night, it was suddenly disturbed by a telephone call from a journalist in the Midlands who happened to be attending a Rita Goold seance. At this point, neither Alf nor Gwen had heard of Rita, nor were they in any way involved in spiritualism. The journalist explained in the telephone call that at the seance they had been given a phone number to call by spirits. A few years ago, Spirit Today published an incredible interview on medium Rita Goold, detailing the remarkable story as it unfolded, and the following day, Alf and Gwen drove to meet the medium themselves. Gwen, takes up the story. "My husband Alf has also joined Russell in Spirit now. Alf and I met in June 1948. Alf passed to spirit in June 2008. The reason I am being interview today is because I have had the rare experience of being reunited with my 'dead' son. Alf and I have met our 'dead' son Russell on many, many occasions; over one hundred, the first being 14 August 1983. I trained to be a classical soprano. I was away singing at Stanstead Hall so I was not home when Alfie took the phone call. He phoned with the news very early the next day. He came and collected me and we drove to the Midlands to sit with a medium that my son Russell had come through with the previous night." As they sat there in the medium's house, Gwen says her son appeared before her. "He was in full form. He held my hands and then his father's hand. There was a lot of "Hello's". He had a torch in his hand which he shone on himself and showed himself fully for us. With his torch, he said to me, "Watch Mum. I will show you all of me!" And he did. The torch was just an ordinary torch, believe me. He started by showing his feet, which were bare; the familiar knees. So familiar to me as I remembered - like any other mother would - the number of times I had scrubbed them. He wore little shorts and a T-shirt. His dear familiar hands with their square nails, just like his daddy. Then up to his face. So beautiful! I can only say that it was just as I had known it. A spirit child is so lovely, one's mind or voice finds it hard to convey a description. There he stood in all his glory! Hair - spiky as always. Eyes - so, so blue - which looked into mine with the love that only a son can share with his mother. How can I explain further? He then took my hand and I was allowed to feel his hair with its familiar cowlick flopping over his dear sweet face. Freckles too, all over his nose. As I have already said, I cannot explain this 'energy', but will leave it to the experts in that particular field. Also, I will not try and describe my feelings at that moment as they are mine only, and now a very precious memory."

Gwen and Alf were not the only parents of a lost child to be reunited. Husband and wife Pat and Barry Jefery's also had the same experience with the medium, though she too was accused of being a fraud by some. "The sittings took place in their home," Gwen explains, "We spent many nights in their house. Pat and Barry's son Michael came

every evening with Russell. Some researchers came too."
A lady called Rose was also reunited with her dead son.
"She was mourning her son Ronald. An accident. We
invited her to our home for a few days. She went alone to
the sittings. She spoke fluent Dutch. She told me that she
had seen and spoken to her own son, and Russell." Gwen
says, "My message is: don't wait until you lose a loved
one. Look, read and learn. Push the door open to Spiritual
Truths."

Rose explained her experience in the same interview; "I
went to Stansted Hall with a friend, every weekend they
have a demonstration, and that is where I met Gwen.
Gwen invited me to her house, and we clicked straight
away. While I was at Gwen's house, she received a
telephone call. It was Rita. She said to Gwen, "You have a
visitor from Holland and it has been said in the circle that
you should bring this lady along". I was very curious; I
had the feeling that I should go. They proceeded to tell me
more about the circle and this made me even more
curious. Eventually I said, Ok, I'll go back to Holland and
ask my boss for a week's holiday. So that's what I did, I
came back to England on the following Friday. After I
arrived, we went to meet Rita. I had no idea what was
going to happen there. They had told me roughly, but you
can't conceive what it's like if you've never had the
experience. Rita gave us a warm welcome. Then we went
to Pat and Barry's house. There I met a journalist from an

English newspaper, Alan Cleaver, and together we examined the room in which the sitting was going to take place to make sure that there was nothing suspicious or that the room was rigged in some way. We did this by checking the walls to make sure they were solid, that there no secret doors or wires present in the room. After doing this we were satisfied that there was nothing unusual about the room. Then they all went into the room – about seven guests and the light was turned off. 'I had no idea of what was about to happen. We were sitting holding hands, there was a small table in the middle with a trumpet and a drum stick on it. I couldn't believe what happened next. The drum stick started flying around the room at such a speed, and with a changing of speed, direction and height, that it was impossible that someone, or some contraption in the room was making this happen, but still I remained sceptical. People have said to me that it was Rita's voice I heard, but that's not possible because I could hear Rita what I can only describe as snoring... I could hear clearly that the voice and the snoring were coming from two different directions, and I heard them at the same time. You can't snore and speak at the same time. The voice I heard wasn't from any of the others sitting in the circle. Russell came through and spoke to me… The sitting progressed; Russell was getting up to mischief. I had things thrown at me - in a playful manner you understand! He threw screwed up tissue and these were meant to be snowballs.'

Although some said Rita Goold was a fake, Alan Crossley, who was also there, and who materialised himself at an Alexander seance after he died, said Russell told him what it was like in the spirit world. "I'm in my life. I carry on like you carry on. My world is as real as yours. I have got a body; well the other body is dead. When we are here, we can change to what we used to be. It's very nice. We have lots of beautiful places, lots of water and flowers that don't die like your flowers. Every flower, every tree that has died is in our world. Everything that has been alive with a life force doesn't die. You can come and visit us but you can't visit us until you are asleep. Some people don't remember. We can come to you in your dreams, more than you can come to us. Don't be frightened. There's nothing to be frightened about. I am still Russell Byrne and I can say I've got brothers and sisters, uncles and cousins and aunts. My Mom's sitting in the chair and she keeps biting her lip. We don't worry like you worry, but we stand at the side and think, don't be like that. We don't like anyone being unhappy but if you cry because you laugh, we love it. But if you cry because you cry, if we could wipe the tears away, we can't always do that...If you are sad, we don't like it. When you are unhappy, we don't like it. One day my Dad threw the cats out of the door, Snowey and Dillon. Next morning, Dad got out of bed, goes in the kitchen and he says, 'Oh my God, what a mess,' and Mom was in bed. She said 'What's the matter now.' She got out of bed, through the room, through the other room, and said, 'Oh my God look at the mess.' The telephone was off the hook, the telephone had fallen on the floor. Well it wasn't Dillon and it wasn't Snowey, it was me. I stood in the kitchen and Dillon saw me and he leaped in the air and jumped in the soil and knocked the phone off. When the cat's hair stands on end, he can see me!"

CHAPTER TEN

"I had the pleasure of seeing a manifestation of Mr W.T. Stead. His body from the waist up, was quite distinct."

A rather humorous account comes from Carl A. Wickland, born in 1861. He was a Doctor, who also wrote, Thirty Years among the Dead, in 1924, which catalogued his experiments in afterlife communication. One part of his investigations involved using his wife to attempt to communicate with the dead through the process of automatic writing. He says, 'My wife proved to be an excellent intermediary and was easily controlled by 'discarnate intelligences.' The spirits apparently told Dr. and Mrs. Wickland, 'There is in reality no death, but a natural transition from the visible to the invisible world, and that advanced spirits are ever striving to communicate with mortals to enlighten them.' Dr. Wickland decided he would use his wife to enable any dead people who wished to, to take over his wife's body in order that he might communicate with them, he explains. One day, when he was still training to become a

Doctor, he went off as usual to a class at the medical college. The body of a 60-year-old man was lying on a slab in front of all the medical students in the laboratory, and Dr. Wickland was going to take part in dissecting the body for their anatomy class. 'I began dissecting on a lower limb,' Dr. Wickland writes. When 5 o'clock came, he made his way back home, where his wife greeted him. 'I had scarcely entered the door, when my wife drew herself up; "What do you mean by cutting me?" I answered I was not aware of cutting anyone. His wife angrily replied, "Of course you are! You are cutting my leg!" Then it clicked; 'Realising that the spirit owner of the body on which I had been operating had followed me home, I began to parley with him. The spirit (through his wife) told him, "I am no woman – I'm a man! Say, Mister, I'm dying for a smoke." Dr. Wickland says, 'This request I of course refused,' and he points out that his wife abhorred the habit of smoking. The following day, Wickland returned to college and his dissection class, and upon observation he noted, 'Subsequent examination of the teeth of the cadaver indicated that the man had been an inveterate tobacco user in life.'

Wickland's strange experiences didn't end there. Next, the body of a 40-year-old woman lay on the dissection table. 'A number of students, myself included, were assigned this subject for dissection. I could not be present the first evening, but the others began. Nothing was ever said to me of what occurred, but for some reason, the other students never touched that subject again.' (By 'subject,' he means the body.) 'The next day, I began to dissect alone, working on the arm and neck. I distinctly heard a voice say, "Don't murder me!" I concluded it probably came from the street. The following afternoon, I was again alone when I was startled by a rustling sound coming from a crumpled newspaper on the floor, a sound like that when a newspaper is crushed. A few days later, we were holding a psychic workshop in our home.' Suddenly, his wife said to him, "I have some bones to pick with you! Why do you want to kill me? You are cutting on my arm and neck. I shouted at you not to murder me. I struck that paper on the floor to frighten you, but you wouldn't pay any attention!" Wickland says that over time, he spoke with more than twenty spirits, 'The majority giving me satisfactory evidence of being certain friends and relatives known to me. In all, they spoke 6 different languages, while my wife speaks only English and Swedish.'

William Thomas Stead was born in 1849. He was a London Newspaper editor who today is considered to be the pioneer of investigative journalism. He was also a campaigner for the rights of the most vulnerable members of society and he petitioned for the improvement of conditions in the slums of London. Tragically, he was aboard the Titanic when it sank. Strangely though, before his death, Stead had written a fictional story called, 'From the Old World to the New,' in which a ship steered by a Captain called Edward J. Smith, (the same name as the Captain of the Titanic) is bound for America when it's sunk by an iceberg. Stead had also written a short story for the Pall Mall Gazette, in which an ocean liner goes down and many lives are lost because there are too few lifeboats, again just like the Titanic. Journalist Roger Luckhurst has described survivor accounts of Stead's last meal on board the Titanic. 'He chatted enthusiastically through the 11-course meal ... telling thrilling tales including one about the cursed mummy in the British Museum, then retired for bed at 10.30 pm.' According to author Joseph O. Baylen, after the Titanic struck the iceberg, Stead helped women and children into lifeboats, and selflessly gave his own life jacket to another passenger. Again, rather oddly, Baylen adds that Stead had often claimed he would be dead, "wither by lynching or drowning." During a public speech three years prior to the disaster, Stead had also drawn a picture of himself as the victim of a shipwreck who is calling for help! In 1920, a memorial was erected for him in Central Park in New York City. It reads, 'Dying nobly, enabled others to live.' New York City Department of Parks and Recreation say, 'He bravely distinguished himself by helping others at the expense of his own life while the Titanic sank into the depths of the North Atlantic. Two allegorical figures flank the inscription, a knight representing Fortitude and an angel representing Sympathy. The knight was stolen in the 1930's and resculpted in 1936.' When Stead was on board the Ship, his daughter was on a national tour with her Shakespearean drama company. One of the members in the group was a young man called Pardoe Woodman. According to Ms. Stead, a few days before the sinking, over a cup of tea, Woodman told her that there was to be a great disaster at sea, and that an elderly man very close to her would be among the victims. Woodman then went off to fight in the Great War, but five years after Stead's death, Woodman began telling those close to him that he was receiving messages from Stead, through the process of automatic writing. Woodman would write out the messages, but then he would often stop and go back to dot the i's and cross the t's. He didn't know it, but this had been a particular habit of Stead's. William Stead had apparently first become interested in Spiritualism in the 1890's, and three years before his death, he had published Letters from Julia. 'Julia' was a spirit who Stead said had begun communicating with him. Her full name was Ms Julia Ames, and she had been an American journalist and Temperance reformer whom Stead had known when she was alive. In 1909, Stead had formed the rather unusual 'Julia's Bureau,' which was a private organisation set up to provide answers from Julia and other spirits about what it was like in the afterlife. Members of the public could write to Stead and his colleagues with questions about life-after-death, and receive answers from the spirits.

After Stead's death, General Sir Alfred Turner reported that he'd held a séance with a medium called Mrs Etta Wriedt, and that he had physically seen Stead. Professor Coates of Rothesay, a well-known author in his day and an investigator of spiritualism also observed, "Mr. Stead showed himself twice within a short time, the last appearance being clearly defined, and none will readily forget the clear, ringing tones of his voice. Mr. Stead has manifested and proved in his own person that the dead do return." The appearance of the dead Stead happened, said Professor Coates, "in our own home and in the presence of fourteen sane and thoughtful people." In fact, Professor Coates would go on to write a book in 1913 called Has Stead returned? The book consisted of a series of accounts from a multitude of witnesses who had physically seen Stead after his death. Professor Coates wrote, 'Mr Stead has manifested on several occasions in our home, having four times etherealized, three times with sufficient clearness for identification, and spoken twice, as only Mr. Stead can speak.' The professor also received correspondence from a number of witnesses including a Vice Admiral Moore, who says in his letter, 'The first appearance of W.T. Stead at Cambridge House, his country residence was at 11.30 am, May 6th when I was sitting in the dark with Mrs Wriedt.' His daughter

Estelle was present at the time. Admiral Moore also describes the appearance of another spirit, a Dr. Sharp, 'who sometimes interrupted what he (Stead) had to say!' At a séance involving the participation of members of 'Julia's Bureau,' Stead appeared once more and so too did 'an Indian' spirit, who told the medium, Mrs Wriedt, that her husband back in Detroit had slipped over while walking up the outside steps to their front door, and had badly sprained his ankle. This was later confirmed to be the case by the receipt of a letter from her husband. 'Julia' herself manifested too, as well as Stead's son who had died before him. Stead's daughter Estelle confirmed that it was her brother's voice and his mannerisms. Another participant at these seances was a Mr. E.R. Sercold Skeels, who also wrote to Professor Coates about seeing Stead materialise. 'I distinctively saw an etherealization of him, head and shoulders, with beard slightly whiter than I remember it.' A Miss Harper was also at the seances. She had been Stead's secretary when he was alive. She wrote, 'My mother and I were both present on May 6th. We saw Mr. Stead absolutely, unmistakably and heard him speak.' A Norwegian journalist called Mrs Anker wrote to Professor Coates, 'Suddenly, W. T. Stead's face appeared in brilliant light... perfectly clear and distinct until it disappeared suddenly... his voice was heard speaking characteristically in his own way.' A Mr. Archibald Bryson, who Professor Coates describes as a well-known level-headed Glasgow merchant, told hm, 'I had the pleasure of seeing a manifestation of Mr W.T. Stead. His body from the waist up, was quite distinct. There was no chance of mistaking the massive head and rugged features and the expressive eyes. He addressed Mrs Jonson and myself; "I am so glad to have the opportunity of coming here and proving to you that I am alive. Make this great truth known." Another witness was a physicist called W. de Kerlor, who had also known Stead. He later wrote, 'The manifestation was so real, the voice so exactly like his when alive, the words and emphatic assertions in every detail so like himself… and the reality of Mr Stead's personality so tangible.' Professor Coates also includes the testimony of a Count Cedo Miyattovich, who was an old friend of Stead's and a former ambassador. Count Miyattovich describes a séance with the medium Mrs Wriedt in Wimbledon, London. The séance began with Mrs Wriedt seated on a chair among the guests, rather than in the cabinet. 'Mr Stead's spirit nodded to me in a friendly manner and disappeared. Half a minute later, he reappeared again and stood opposite me but somewhat higher than above the floor, looking at me, bowing at me. We all three heard distinctly, "Yes, I am Stead – William Stead! And my dear friend, Miyattovich, I am so pleased you came here – I came here to bring you proof of what I was telling you, that you should not only believe but know that there really is a life after death…"

CHAPTER ELEVEN

"We had a full height, full materialization of a person that was fully recognized by the details of their dress and their mannerisms."

Medium Gordon Higginson was born in Longton, Staffordshire in 1918. He would go on to become President of the Spiritualists' National Union (the SNU), as well as Principal of the Arthur Findlay College of Spiritualism and Psychic sciences. His mother Fanny Higginson had also been a medium. Longton Spiritualist Church describe her as 'a very strong lady, outspoken and hard working.' In fact, she would go on to serve as a medium in the Church there for seventy years. They say, 'Fanny possessed a unique gift of mediumship often displaying physical and trance mediumship.' Fanny first visited Longton Spiritualist Church at the age of 14 with her aunt Mrs Taylor, and their visit could not have been more dramatic. 'Fanny was given a message by medium Annie Brittain which would change her life,' says the Church. The message was that Fanny would have a son who would become a world-famous platform medium, and that her own future lay in the development of trance mediumship. This wasn't the dramatic bit though; there was more, and it was the next part of the message that was so shocking. 'Fanny was told that Annie had a spirit with her who was also named Fanny and was in fact the 14-year old's mother.' On hearing this, Fanny replied that this was impossible: she had just left her mother at home only an hour earlier. The medium however advised Fanny to return home immediately. 'On her arrival, Fanny was devastated that her mother had indeed passed away.' Her mother had literally died of a heart attack while Fanny had been at the Spiritualist Church. As Fanny went on to become a medium herself, they say, 'Recipients described the evidence given as "life changing." In fact, a famous mining company would not dig test bores without consulting her, so accurate was her advice.' Fanny's son, Gordon Higginson also became a medium too, as had been foretold all those years ago. He became widely known for his highly accurate messages, although there were occasions when his work was questioned, as has been the case for most mediums through the ages. Parapsychologist Dr. Barrie Colvin wrote about Gordon in Psypioncer Magazine following a British newspaper investigation into the medium in the 1970's. Professor Colvin had attended one of Gordon's séances at the famous Arthur Findlay College in Stanstead. The séance room had been set-up by the organisers, then there was half an hour or so before it was due to start. Colvin later wrote, 'I had no difficulty at all in walking into and out of the seance room during the course of the next half-hour. During a brief visit to the room, I quickly felt under the seat covering of each of the chairs in the front row…I decided to start at the centre of the row and work outwards.' As he did so, he found something suspicious. 'Within just a few seconds I had discovered a large quantity of muslin-like material tightly wrapped and placed underneath the seat of the end chair.' As the séance got underway, Colvin says he was invited by a spirit to approach the cabinet and feel the ectoplasm. 'Clearly it had the feel of the fabric I had discovered… It was a truly disappointing end to an investigation,' he concludes. Colvin believed this was obviously quite clearly a case of cheating. Many others who investigated Gordon disagreed however.

During Gordon's seances he would go into the cabinet, and according to many witnesses over the decades, spirit materialisations often happened; but Colvin had not been impressed by the séance he attended and he believed he had uncovered trickery very swiftly. This wasn't his first experience with Gordon. He'd had also attended an earlier demonstration at Eltham Spiritualist Church in March 1974, accompanied by a Brigadier Frank Spedding. Both Colvin and Spedding were members of the Society for Psychical Research, the SPR. Of this experience, Colvin wrote, 'During the course of the sitting, certain figures appeared from time to time a foot or so in front of the cabinet. As I closely examined the spirit form, albeit in dim light, I could clearly make out the features of the medium and I had no doubt that the figure standing before me consisted of a normal light material such as cotton draped over the medium's physical form. Frank Spedding came to exactly the same conclusion.' In Spedding's report for the SPR, he wrote, 'Our opinion was that the materialisations were crude fakes which should not have deceived anyone of normal intelligence.' Unfortunately, fakery in physical mediumship has happened since the Victorian era when the roots of spiritualism began, and even up to recent times with the exposure of a contemporary medium called Gary Mannion, as I mentioned earlier. Fraudulent mediums have been the bane of Physical mediumship, to the extent that today there are very few mediums even willing to attempt physical mediumship for fear of being accused of cheating, and physical mediumship is generally regarded as a laughing stock by the general public because of the frauds and con-artists who have given it this reputation. Perhaps the answer as to why some mediums or pretend mediums have been tempted to impersonate the materialisation of dead people is because they can make money out of it, but also because it elevates their standing as "the best" mediums. Any medium performing a demonstration to an audience, be it on a platform or at a séance, is also under pressure to "perform;" to show the audience the evidence they are so desperate for – and what they have paid for. Many mediums I have spoken with in my research, and some who I have come to know very well now, have said there will always be the odd occasion where nothing happens; no spirits come to give messages. An ethical and honest, genuine medium will draw the séance or demonstration to a close and explain this. Fake or unscrupulous mediums will try to bluff it. However, they should know that any mediums sitting in the audience, or having a reading from them will know they are faking it – because they can 'link in' to what the medium says they are seeing! Famous mediums through the ages have perhaps bent to the pressure of audience expectation and for this reason, they have faked spirit materialisation evidence too, like the accusation against Gordon Higginson of using muslin to pretend it's ectoplasm, or dressing up as dead people and parading around the room. Unfortunately, this has ruined genuine physical mediumship. In the Victorian era, fraudulent mediums even used faces cut out of magazines and newspapers to pretend these were spirit faces in photographs of seances. Having got to know a number of contemporary mediums of good repute and excellent mediumistic abilities, who have personally seen physical mediums working, they have told me that some of the past mediums, well-known in the spiritualist movement, who have been exposed as frauds often had genuine mediumship abilities, which they witnessed personally; yet these mediums were also prone on occasion to faking it too, which muddies the waters even more. It really isn't cut and dried. How do these mediums I have talked to know this? Real mediums can see what is genuine and what is not clairvoyantly, clairsentiently, and so on, and they can see whether the medium in question is really in trance or is simply delusional, or is outright cheating. For the average audience-goer however, with no clairvoyant abilities, it is so much harder to know what is real.

In the case of Gordon Higginson, given that he presided at the Spiritualists' National Union, an organisation replete with very genuine mediums, and having also held the position of Principal of the foremost college for mediums, Gordon Higginson surely would have been found out immediately, had he been faking his abilities? And, in contrast to Colvin and Spedding's opinion of Gordon, former tutor at the Arthur Findlay College, as well as being one of the world's leading spiritual healers, Steven Upton has told me that he personally used to search Gordon Higginson before demonstrations at the College, and he attests that the physical materialisations he witnessed were absolutely real.

Proof of the Afterlife

Paul Challenger interviews a Reverend Arthur Plumpton on the Gordon Higginson tribute website, run by medium Martin Twycross. Plumpton says, "I think the most dramatic experience I've had was certainly with Gordon Higginson, the President of the SNU from 1970 up until 1993. He did frequent visits to the Arthur Findlay College and on one occasion we were there for his physical phenomena week... a physical circle with Gordon in his cabinet. One day, necessary cleaning processes were went through and the pre-circle processes where he bathed and was inspected, and all the security things went forwards in order to minimize the possibility of cheating. That particular evening, we were in the front row in reduced lighting. We had the direct voice from his helpers, (he means spirit voices were heard; those of Gordon's spirit guides, speaking independently, not through Gordon's mouth), "and eventually we got a physical apparition and you could see the ectoplasm form and flow, and for the first time you're absolutely amazed – you're gob-smacked that this is actually happening in front of your eyes. We had a full height, full materialization of a person that was fully recognized by the details of their dress and their mannerisms, recognized by the tone of their voice, and recognized also by the detail that was given to the recipient. I found it absolutely fascinating that what I'd read about in books actually happened in front of my eyes. I've always said since that day; once you've seen it there's no turning back. I still see it in my mind's eye… it really was a physical phenomenon event, and it reminds me of the intelligence that spirit have and continue to use to try to help us in this world." Reverend Plumpton describes the materialised spirit. "It was dark purple, a dress like a ball gown, a female, recognised and accepted as a relative from the visual appearance and the evidence that was given." Could he have been fooled? Was this Gordon Higginson dressed up as a woman, and somehow looking exactly like the dead relative of an audience member? But how could that be when he didn't know the people in the audience personally, nor their families? Reverend Plumpton says, "It built from the ground upwards," which surely makes it impossible for this figure to have been Gordon himself! If Gordon had been putting ectoplasm, which Colvin said he had once retrieved a sample of from the back pocket of a chair seat in the audience, and thrown it around his body, while also changing into a ladies ballgown and somehow making his face look like someone's dead relative, how could he have done this by building "from the ground upwards?" Not only that, but if Reverend Plumpton could see the materialised spirit "build", then how could he not have seen Gordon putting on a dress and somehow changing his face too? And if Gordon built up from the floor, how did he manage to make most of his body vanish, in order for it then to build up? Reverend Plumpton adds,

"Gordon Higginson was also fully visible at the same time. The apparition was visible for a few minutes, and held a conversation." It obviously wasn't Gordon dressed up then. Could it have been someone else dressed up? It's possible; but to cheat like that at the top psychic college in the world, with very experienced mediums in the audience, would have been career suicide and a humiliating public exposure, leaving his reputation in tatters.

The medium Paul Jacobs, who was tutored by Gordon, once made an interesting comment to Psychic News, "One thing that's very popular today is two evidential mediums communicating with the same spirit person at the same time. I first did this 30 years ago – it was something Gordon Higginson made us do in our training. It came in handy when I began teaching, so I could link-in to a student's contact and follow them, something I believe all teachers of mediumship should be able to." This happens in my home circle in South West London. The two mediums who teach us can see what we are seeing, they can see the spirits who are communicating with us during our exercises, by 'linking-in', like Jacobs has described Gordon doing. Gordon used the same method of teaching as my tutors; so, if Gordon had 'linked in' and described the spirits who were communicating with his students, at least some of the students would have known if he was getting it wrong or was simply making it up and faking it!

My tutors can see the spirit communicating with me and can describe them and it matches what I'm seeing. They can say who the spirit is in relation to the partner I'm working with, and can see, for example, if a spirit has taken me into their house where they lived when they were alive, and if they are showing me their kitchen, or a study filled with books. For example, we were working in pairs and the object of the exercise was to try to get spirit communication from a deceased family member of my partner. I seemed to be getting information from my partner's deceased father. He took me to his house, I could see the living room, the furniture, the book shelves, the paintings on the wall, as well as the kitchen. My tutor asked me to describe out loud what I was seeing. I described that one of the paintings was of a horse's head. This was confirmed to be accurate by my partner, the spirit's daughter. I described seeing him sitting down reading a broadsheet newspaper, which she again confirmed that he was in the habit of doing. My tutor asked what else I could see. I said I could see that lots of the books on his bookshelf were about birds. Again, his daughter confirmed that he did have a lot of bird books. He showed me his kitchen, from the vantage point of the living room, and I could see an open hatch between the living room and kitchen, which his daughter said had been present in their house. I could then see he was showing me a jam jar, with writing on the cover of it. My tutor asked me what the writing said, but I could not make it out clearly. He however could, and told us what it said. My point in saying all this, is to demonstrate that like Gordon Higginson, my tutor also links in to what spirit are showing me, and my tutor was seeing the same thing as me, except much more clearly than I, because his abilities are so much greater than mine. When we do our meditation exercise, we begin by being led in it by our tutor. In one class, we were led through a field into a forest and our tutor described things for us to see in the forest. After a few minutes of being guided like this, we are then left there to try to connect with spirits. On this occasion, I had somehow found myself wandering off to a beach. After the exercise ended, my tutor was laughing, and asked me what I had been doing on a beach! They had linked into me and seen what I was doing, and they do the same with all the students. In another exercise, I seemed to be getting communication from a spirit and I asked them lots of questions, in my mind. After the exercise, my tutor asked me why I had asked a specific question – again, demonstrating that they had linked in during my spirit communication. If I don't get any spirit contact, and I am a mere beginner, I will always immediately tell my tutor. It would be pointless to make things up, tempting though that might be, to save my embarrassment, particularly when we have to give readings in front of the class and all eyes are on me. The anxiety inside me builds and builds, and I feel the pressure to "perform", because everyone is staring at me and they're all so good at it, and the knot in my stomach gets tighter, and I almost go into a panic that no spirits are going to come, and the feeling of letting everyone down sweeps over me; so I can almost understand why sometimes experienced medium might be tempted to cheat or try to trick their audience; except that, they are often dealing with very vulnerable and bereaved people who come to them full of hope, and that is so cruel. Anyway, in my case, if I tried to cheat, my tutors would know I was!

That Gordon Higginson possessed genuine mediumistic skills was proven time and time again in his platform demonstrations, as can be seen in the following accounts. The 1959 December issue of Psychic News describes a 'Mystery Test' they carried out on Gordon. Present for this test was Charles Quastel, President of the SNU, along with others from the head of the Union, including the Secretary, Richard Ellidge. It took place at the Spiritualist Church in Belper in the Derbyshire Hills. The purpose, they say was, 'To have on permanent record an absolutely exact record of all the evidence provided in a normal church demonstration, complete with statements by all the recipients of messages and confirmed by them in personal interviews after the service,' and secondly, 'To ensure public confidence in the mediumship of Gordon Higginson and other remarkable mediums.' In preparation for the service, Gordon was not told the location of the Church until an hour before it he was due to begin, and it had already been established that he had never been to this Church before. Neither had any of those officiating the test either. The members of the Spiritualist Church were not told who the medium coming would be until a few days before the evening. Of course, in those days there were no mobile phones nor the internet; Gordon would not have been able to find out about the audience by going on Facebook, for example, to look for clues about their life and their families; and besides which, he did not know who was going to be there anyway. Gordon duly arrived and gave his platform demonstration, and immediately afterwards, Quastel spoke to those in the audience who had received messages, to establish whether they were accurate or not. He later wrote, 'To say that the congregation was literally gasping with amazement at the wealth of evidential detail is no exaggeration.' The evidence given by Gordon was collected during the service by a Mrs. E. Coleman of the visiting SNU, who wrote her notes verbatim. At one point during the demonstration, Gordon asks the audience, "You know Mrs. Bako or Varo?" Someone in the audience replies, "Yes," and Gordon continues, "Did she go to another Church other than a Spiritual Church? She is giving me the name Reverend Thomas. She would know him quite well." "Yes," the same person, a female audience member replies, "There were two Churches connected. She would know the Rev. Thomas." Gordon then asks, "Mrs. Cartwright – lived at St Peter's. Her name was Gertie?" "Yes," replies the same woman. "Did she not live in Church Street?" asks Gordon. "Yes". Gordon continues, "She is telling me that where she used to live is all 'poshed up' now." "Yes," the lady confirms. Gordon says, "She says they have painted the houses where she lived green." "Yes," agrees the woman. "She was born in number four and died in number two," says Gordon. "Quite correct," says the lady in the audience. In another message Gordon asks the audience, "Hannah or Annie? She tells me that she often stood at the door and watched people go past?" A different member of the audience confirms that this is correct. Gordon continues, "She tells me they used to have a bit of a garden in front of their place and she used to stand there as if she owned the lot, but she did not. It belonged to Four Houses." "Yes," the audience member confirms again. "There was a butcher's shop nearby," says Gordon, "and during the war she could see the meat arriving. Used to go and bang on the door saying, "It's no good putting it under the counter and saying you have none – I have just seen it come!" The audience member laughs, "Yes, that is correct." In another message, Gordon tells the audience, "Young man here who was drowned. He was in a boat with a friend named Tony. Boat overturned?" "Yes," a man in the audience replies, "I know his father. I work with his father." Gordon continues, "His name is Colin Michael Richards. His friend was Tony Creswell." "Quite correct," affirms the man. The Secretary of the SNU, Quastel ends his report with the comment, 'A noticeable feature of modern literature relating to spiritual activities and Church practices is the regrettable omission of full details of evidence provided by mediums in normal spiritualist services,' and this is quite true. In my local area alone, there are at least 6 Spiritualist Churches within a 5-mile radius, who usually hold twice-weekly services where a multitude of messages from spirit are given to members of the public in the audiences, which they confirm to be correct and accurate. Having attended many of these services, it's obvious that the audience members are not known to the mediums, as often people have never been to these types of services before and they are open to the general public to simply walk in; yet this evidence of spirit communication never really goes any further than word of mouth, when stunned visitors go home and inevitably tell their family and friends about what happened. So seldom do these amazing accounts ever get out into wider circulation, which is such a shame.

In 1969, ATV television channel interviewed Gordon and filmed him as he gave a public demonstration. The TV reporter, Alan Jones, seen standing outside Gordon's Spiritualist Church in Longton says, "While other churches in the district here remain empty on Sundays, this one here, Longton Spiritualist Church, is full. They're turning people away." Gordon and the congregation are being filmed as he gives his demonstration. He says to the audience, "It seems to me one would have to go back into their very young life to find this name, and I seem to be somewhere where there may be a small shop. I heard he (the spirit) was to do with a cat that died in the yard and there was a terrible fuss about this cat because the person wouldn't accept that it hadn't been poisoned." A lady in the audience speaks up. "Oh, that's right," she says, "Yes! She was very upset about this cat!" Gordon continues, saying, "Because didn't she say this wasn't natural - somebody had poisoned it?" "Yes," says the lady, "Somebody had poisoned it, that's right, yes." The reporter interviews Gordon afterwards, who explains that from a young age, at two or three years old, he could see spirit people. "Spiritualism has had so much criticism from people who do not know anything about it. Lots of people believe they are in contact with the spirit world when they are not. But it doesn't take away, there are millions of people that have been convinced. Healers, who have this particular gift, it is a question of getting a closeness with the spirit and working with them." The reporter then interviews a former patient of Gordon, a Mrs. Jones, who says she had rheumatoid arthritis when she came to him for healing. "In my hands, shoulders, knees, feet," she says. The reporter asks her if she had seen her doctor about the condition before she came to Gordon. "Oh yes," she says, "and I was under the hospital too." "Were they making you better?" "No," she says. "I don't know what I was expecting really. I came hoping." After her first healing session with Gordon she says, "I could lift my arm up and that's not something I had been able to do for two years." The reporter asks her, "Do you live a normal, active life now?" "Yes, I do all my own housework and everything." Another lady called Mrs. Ray is also interviewed about Gordon's healing work. She says, "Well, of course, I couldn't walk, I was carried in. Curvature of the spine, kidneys and heart and rheumatoid arthritis." She says she came for healing for a period of 6 months, getting better over the duration. "As time went on, I gradually got so I could stand, and then I could walk a little, then I could get about the home. Then I went into business and I had two shops!"

Gordon can also be seen in a video clip from the SNU giving a platform demonstration. He asks a woman in the audience, "Who is William?" The woman replies, "My husband." Gordon says, "He's got a lovely place waiting for you. Twelve months ago, you weren't very well?" "That's correct, yes," she replies. "Well," says Gordon, "Do you know, he was rubbing his hands hoping you were going." What Gordon means here is that her husband was hoping she was going to die and enter the afterlife to be with him! The woman laughs and says, "I wouldn't mind!" Gordon continues, "He was hoping so because he's rubbing his hands and saying she's not very well at all, she really wishes sometimes that she was with me and with the family." "Yes," says the woman, "That's true, that's true." Gordon continues, "Because they've nearly all gone now, haven't they?" "Yes," the woman confirms. Gordon asks, "There's only 3 of you left?" "Yes, that's right." "Yes," says Gordon, "He's just said so now. He's talking about Mr. Kitchen and then he says you've left Mrs. Kitchen behind and she used to be around you, is that right?" "Yes," confirms the woman. "She used to speak about Mr. Stead?" "Yes." "Well, they've met Mr. Stead on the other side and now they've spoken about Mrs. Stead. Do you understand that?" "Yes," replies the woman, "I've been talking to her daughter the other day..." Of course, Gordon Higginson had never met this woman in the audience, and he could not possibly have known these personal details about how she was feeling and who her friends were.

Eric Hatton, former president of the SNU also mentions a remarkable incident involving Gordon in his own autobiography, Taking up the challenge. Hatton's book, says the SNU, 'is the story of one man's determination to find an answer to the question we will all ask at some time or another - is there life after death? When Eric Hatton's much-loved brother was killed in 1946, he was determined to embark on his own investigation. Thus, began a quest for evidence.' Hatton's search lasted 60 years. He was a busy, successful businessman at the same time, and this, says the SNU, 'meant that his feet have always been planted firmly on the ground.' Before we get to the relevance of Gordon, Hatton describes a curious incident in his autobiography. He explains that when his brother was home on leave from the military, he would talk about his experiences in Catalina flying boats, an amphibious aircraft made in the 30's and 40's. Hatton says, 'One night my brother related a strange tale. He told us that in some of the flying boats both he and other crew members had 'seen' colleagues who had been killed in aircraft accidents.' Hatton says, 'In essence, it seemed that although these fellows were dead, they were actually walking along the gangway of the plane.' Even stranger, 'These dead fellows would walk straight through my brother... and through other crew members.' Hatton was very scornful of his brother's tale, and in response his brother challenged Hatton to do some investigation of his own to find out if what his brother was saying could really be true. Shortly after this, just before demob in 1946, Hatton's brother was away serving in Singapore when his plane crashed into the sea, killing him. Hatton received a telegram telling him of his brother's death. Weeks passed by, with Hatton and the rest of his family struggling to cope with their grief, and here we get to Gordon, because,

'Then,' says Hatton, 'out of the blue, a letter dropped onto the doormat.' It was from the Secretary of Longton Spiritualist Church, where Gordon Higginson gave his demonstrations, although Hatton had no idea who he was at the time, having never heard of him or the Church. The letter told Hatton, 'the extraordinary news that my brother had manifested during one of Gordon's circles.' His brother's name was given in the letter, along with his nickname, 'that only my sister and I ever called him – "Kim." In addition, we were given his full service number,' (his long military personal identification number) as well as 'the circumstances of his death, the way in which his plane had crashed into the sea, and the fact that he had not survived but other crew members had – details that had not been offered to us by the Air Ministry.'

CHAPTER TWELVE

'One Christmas Eve, a stranger suddenly appeared before him, though the door was closed.'

When Queen Victoria withdrew from public life following the death of her husband Prince Albert, is it possible that she continued to communicate with him? After the Queen lost her beloved husband, she insisted that his room must be kept exactly as if he were still alive. Every evening, a clean nightshirt, fresh flowers and a jug of hot water were laid out in his room. By preserving every semblance of his existence, the Queen must have felt she could try to keep his presence alive, as though he had not really gone. His death had plunged her into a grief so overwhelming that her courtiers feared she would lose her mind. Above all, the Queen longed to hear his voice again. And, so it was that in the very room in which he had died, she took part in a séance, accompanied by her Highland ghillie John Brown and close trusted courtiers. Together, they sat in the dark and waited. Sometime later, through the darkness a man's voice came. The voice was coming from John Brown's mouth, but it was not Brown's gruff and heavy Scottish brogue anymore. Instead, the Queen recognised the unmistakable voice of her dear husband Albert, talking to her from beyond the grave about things only she knew.

The seance had been organised after a series of strange events had occurred. It all began shortly after her husband's death, when in Birmingham, hundreds of miles away, a Mr. and Mrs. Lees were having a private séance in their living room. During the evening, a voice came from the Lees' teenage son, Robert James, saying that he was "Albert, the Prince Consort." The voice asked that his wife the Queen be told that although he was dead, he could still communicate with her through the body of this 13-year-old boy! The editor of a local newspaper happened to be at the séance. He was a family friend, and after hearing Robert Lees give the message purporting to be from Prince Albert, he went ahead and published an account of it in the newspaper.

It was not long before the Queen herself came to hear of the story, and she was so intrigued that she responded by instructing two of her courtiers to go to the home of Robert Lees to investigate. So, the courtiers duly set off to attend the next séance held at the Lees home in Birmingham, and upon arrival they gave fake names to ensure that no connection to the Queen could be established. As the séance began, it was not long before Robert Lees appeared once again to be communicating with Prince Albert, and Albert had a direct message for the two visitors, calling them by their real names too. It would not have been possible for the 13-year-old boy to know the names of the Queen's private courtiers. Not only this, but the boy gave them a Freemason's handshake, indicating that he was aware they were Freemasons. Then he proceeded to tell the men some very personal and private details about themselves, which he could not possibly have known about, and he told them very directly that he knew they had been sent by Queen Victoria.

Robert James Lees, born in 1849, had always felt different. He seemed to have the ability to speak to the dead. The boy relayed information to the courtiers which would later be proven by the Queen to be correct and only known between her and Prince Albert. When the courtiers returned to the Palace, the Queen was eager to find out what had happened. They told her all about it, and they handed her a letter that the boy Lees had written to her. The letter was signed in a name used only by the Prince when he was talking privately to the Queen – a name that only she knew. As a result, the Queen became so convinced the boy had been communicating with her dead husband that she immediately sent a request for Robert Lees to come to the Palace and reside there permanently as her personal medium in order that she may talk to her husband at all times. However, young Lees turned down this offer from her Majesty. We do have confirmation of this happening from several sources including a curious letter sent by Sir Arthur Conan Doyle on November the 6th 1928, in which he says, 'Dear Mr. Lees, I was wondering whether the remarkable story of the late Queen and your psychic experiences could not be put on record - even if it were not publicly used. It seems to me, so far as I understand it, to be a point of great historical interest. The general outline as it reached me was that as a young Medium you got a message from Prince A. That you sent it. That two Court Officials came to investigate. That they got messages. That these messages indicated JB (John Brown) as having the same powers as you, and that from then onwards JB did act as medium. We are all growing older & it would be good to leave a clear record behind. Yours sincerely, A Conan Doyle.' As the letter mentions, when Robert Lees politely declined the Queen's offer, he did suggest an alternative solution: that her Highland ghillie John Brown, a servant, was also able to receive messages from her dead husband. He said that Prince Albert had told him this. John Brown was clairvoyant too, said Lees.

As for Robert Lees, he went on to become a writer for the Manchester Guardian and a successful spiritual lecturer. Meanwhile, the Queen immediately sent for her servant John Brown to join her at her Balmoral Estate in the Highlands of Scotland, and soon the pair would become inseparable. Their relationship would cause quite a stir; they became so close that it was a great concern to her advisers and to her grown-up children too. There was speculation among them that this unorthodox relationship between the Queen and her servant, who had formerly taken care of her horses, was of a romantic nature. Queen Victoria had withdrawn from public life following her husband's death and now she and John Brown were always to be found in each other's company. Brown was a big burly bearded outdoorsman who came from the working class. He greatly enjoyed drinking whiskey and smoking. This was not a suitable man to be seen in the company of the Queen! She even let him smoke in her company, when her own sons were forbidden from doing so. She insisted on having him by her side at all times, and she allowed the kind of intimacy that would normally only be granted to a husband, not a servant! Brown slept in an adjoining bedroom to the Queen; far removed from the etiquette according a Royal and her position as Head of State. Many of her other servants called him, "The Queen's stallion," and her children referred to him as "Mamma's lover." There has even been the claim that the Queen married him! In 2003, The Telegraph newspaper wrote, 'There has been speculation for more than 100 years that Queen Victoria had an affair with Mr Brown. There were rumours at the time that the couple married but never any evidence for the claim. Victoria did become Mrs Brown. Newly published diaries provide the most compelling evidence yet that Queen

Victoria married John Brown, her devoted servant in a secret ceremony.' The newspaper explains, 'The diaries of Lewis Harcourt, a politician and minister in Prime Minister Asquith's government claims that the Reverend Norman McLeod, the Queen's Chaplain, made a deathbed confession that he married the couple and regretted it for the rest of his life.' In Harcourt's diaries he wrote, 'Lady Ponsonby (the wife of the Queen's private secretary) told HS (the Home Secretary - the author's father) a few days ago that Miss McLeod declares that her brother Norman MacLeod confessed to her on his deathbed that he married the Queen to John Brown and added that he always bitterly regretted it.' Harcourt reflects on this; 'Miss McLeod could have had no object in inventing such a story so that one is almost inclined to believe it, improbable and disgraceful as it sounds.' Of course, we only have this on the word of one lady. Retired civil servant – turned – author, Patrick Jackson read all 74 of the leather- bound diaries. "The diaries were written for Hardcourt's own personal satisfaction, with no idea of publication or circulation, and no retrospective corrections. I suppose some people would say that it's no more than tittle-tattle but it's certainly very high level gossip from very respectable sources who have no reason to make it up." 'In light of this new 'evidence,' says The Telegraph, 'Many historians still hold the belief that it's highly unlikely and very improbable that the Queen would have married such a lowly man. Whether or not the Queen married her ghillie, and the odds are that she would not have done so, there was great concern that Brown was advising her on issues that he had no authority to do so, and that the Queen would listen to his opinions very seriously.' And now we get to the spiritual part; we do know that she believed she was speaking to her deceased husband through John Brown. The magistrate and spiritualist Sir Arthur Findlay was probably the first person involved in spiritualism to write about the fact that Queen Victoria had communicated with Robert Lees, the teenage medium. In his 1956 book Curse of Ignorance, Volume II, Findlay writes, 'The information was given to the author (Findlay) by his daughter Eva Lees with permission. This is the first occasion that all the facts have been made public. A fact worthy of mention, and one which is quite unknown to historians, is the interest Queen Victoria took in Spiritualism. And this is how it happened. While the Lees family was having a private sitting in their own home, Lees was controlled by a man from the other world who gave the name of Albert, the Prince Consort. He then made the request that Queen Victoria be told that he could communicate with her through this boy medium. She sent anonymously two members of her Court to the home of Lees, who requested that they might have a sitting with him.'

Findlay then goes on to relate how servant John Brown ended up living with the Queen. Her husband, speaking through Lees, 'told the Queen that he could speak to her equally well, and just as easily, by using the vocal organs of the son of a gillie on the Balmoral estate whose name was John Brown. The Queen immediately sent for Brown, and thus began the long and strange friendship of Queen Victoria with John Brown, who, up to his death, was used as the medium of the Prince Consort to communicate with his wife, whom he advised on many questions until her death.' Findlay also provides more detail about Robert Lees. 'The acquaintance of the Queen with Lees did not end with their first meeting, in fact it continued throughout her life-time. Shortly before she died, she sent for Lees and thanked him for all he had done for her. From time to time she offered him honours, a comfortable annuity for his life-time, and gifts, all of which he refused. He would take nothing, he said, in return for his services.' Findlay also expands upon how the Queen's spiritualism impacted those around her; 'The Queen, knowing the prejudice there was at Court, and by the Church towards everything relating to Spiritualism, never wrote to Lees and always sent her messages by a special courier, but she kept a record of all that transpired at her sittings with both John Brown and Lees. The Dean of Windsor, Dr. Davidson, who became Archbishop of Canterbury, was hostile but she quite ignored his advice to discontinue her communications with her husband.' After John Brown died, 'the Queen wrote a monograph about him and wished to publish it. Dr. Davidson and Sir Henry Ponsonby, her Private Secretary objected, the former threatening to resign his position as Court Chaplain.' The Head of her Church at Windsor Castle was indignant, it would seem, and he found the Queen's commitment to communing with the dead unbearable! 'Ponsonby destroyed Brown's diaries so that what was written would never become known. The two Court officials prevented the Queen from publicly testifying to the comfort she had received from the communications.' There are further details in the more contemporary book The Secret History of the Spirit World, written by J.H. Brennan, who says that after Queen Victoria's death, her personal doctor Sir James Reid was forced to intervene 'in a case of blackmail involving a cache of 300 "most compromising" letters' she had written to her estate manager at Balmoral, in which she reportedly discussed her interest in communicating with the other world through Brown. 'Sir James purchased the letters on behalf of her son Edward VII, who destroyed them.' However, according to Brennan, some of Brown's writings may have survived. Brennan says that King George VI once mentioned to his speech therapist Lionel Logue, who he saw in an attempt to conquer his stammer, that he had seen a record of the séances the Queen held in Brown's diaries.

Michael Roll, who runs The Campaign for Philosophical Freedom: secular scientific case for survival after death, asks, 'Why were Queen Victoria's diaries destroyed and then re-written? The current Queen, says Roll, 'let the cat out of the bag during a live TV broadcast – the Queen was seen showing Neil Kinnock (former Labour Prime Minister) and other MP's around Buckingham Palace. Mr Kinnock remarked that it was great to see Queen Victoria's diaries. The Queen tells the truth that Queen Victoria's diaries had all been destroyed because she had upset the British establishment. The diaries were all rewritten, taking out the most important bits where the Queen recorded every sitting she had with her medium John Brown where she made contact with Prince Albert.' Roll says, 'Even those outside the religion of Spiritualism are beginning to realise just how badly they are being deceived by a handful of tyrants, acting as sort of thought police deciding what information is safe to allow through to the public.'

Of Robert Lees, who began Queen Victoria's journey into spiritualism, his eldest daughter Eva has written, 'Before he was twelve years of age, he was a deep trance medium,' and she said he could talk with ease at just 13 on 'a range of philosophic knowledge that astounded his listeners.' His daughter says he was a healer too, who carried out 'remarkable healings.' Eva also adds another intriguing piece of information. 'Robert Lees only claimed to be the amanuensis.' In other words, he was simply one who takes dictation. 'One Christmas Eve, a stranger suddenly appeared before him, though the door was closed. Lees quickly surmised that this was a visitor from the next world and invited him to be seated.' The 'stranger' then proceeded to dictate to Lees as he wrote down all the words, and eventually he published them in a book called Through the Mists, which describes in detail what the Spirit World is like. 'His publication created tremendous interest and it is now in its nineteenth edition,' his daughter says. Incidentally, she also mentions that her father became good friends with Thomas Edison, and 'was one of the first to have his voice recorded.'

American Thomas Alva Edison became known as the man who invented the electric light, the phonograph, and the motion picture camera, although some say this was actually invented by Frenchman Louis le Prince, who mysteriously vanished. What most people possibly don't know is that Edison was also busy working away in his laboratory attempting to build a very mysterious device that he hoped would make it possible to communicate with the dead. But where is this device? In the October 1920 issue of The American magazine, Edison said, "If our personality survives, then it is strictly logical or scientific to assume that it retains memory, intellect, other faculties, and knowledge that we acquire on this Earth. I am inclined to believe that our personality hereafter will be able to affect matter. If this reasoning be correct, then, if we can evolve an instrument so delicate as to be affected by our personality as it survives in the next life, such an instrument, when made available, ought to record something." Edison was 73 years of age at the time and he said, "I have been at work for some time building an apparatus to see if it is possible for personalities which have left this earth to communicate with us." Researcher and writer Stacy Horn, when looking further into Edison's life for her book Unbelievable, says that he also told a Boston Globe reporter, "Man is not the unit of life. The unit of life consists of swarms of billions of highly organized entities which live in the cells. I believe at times that when man dies, this swarm deserts the body, goes out into space, but keeps on and enters another and last cycle of life and is immortal." To the owner of Forbes magazine Edison said, "If this is ever accomplished it will be accomplished not by any occult, mystifying, mysterious or weird means, such as are employed by so-called mediums, but by scientific methods." This was around the time that Sir Arthur Conan Doyle was diving deep into the new spiritualist movement with gusto, while his very good friend Harry Houdini was actively trying to debunk charlatans in the movement. Staff Writer for Forbes, Kristin Tablang writes in a retrospective, 'If successful Edison's electric ghost machine would be able to detect the personalities of the deceased, allowing them to relay messages from the spirit realm.' "I am hopeful," Edison had said, "that by providing the right kind of instrument, we can receive intelligent messages from it in its changed habitation." In the New York Times in 1921, Edison was reported to be developing a machine that would measure "one hundred trillion life units" in the human body that "may scatter after death." After all these reports about Edison's activities, the editor of Scientific American received hundreds of letters from curious readers enquiring about Edison's device. In the October 1933 edition of Modern Mechanix magazine they wrote, 'Amazing Edison's Secret experiments: For thirteen years, results of Edison's astounding attempt to penetrate that wall that lies beyond mortality have been withheld from the world, but now the amazing story can be told.' The article described a secret gathering of a select group of anonymous scientists that had taken place a decade earlier at Edison's laboratory; 'One black, howling wintry night in 1920 – just such a night when superstitious people would bar their doors and windows against marauding ghosts – Thomas Edison, the famous inventive wizard, gathered a small group of scientists in his laboratory to witness his secret experiments to lure spirits from beyond the grave and trap them with instruments of incredible sensitivity. Until recently only a few favoured spectators ever knew what unearthly forms materialized in the laboratory that night to give proof …. but now the amazing story can be told.' The secret experiment, they said, took place, 'In a darkened room surrounded with generators and other experimental equipment. When the experiment was ready to begin, spiritualists in the group were called upon to summon from eternity the ethereal form of its inhabitants and command the spirit to walk across the beam. The scientists watched intently the meter of the electric eye, which would flicker the instant any ghostly form interrupted the light beam.' Edison's equipment included, 'A photo-electric cell,' and he used, 'A tiny pencil of light, coming from a powerful lamp,' which 'bored through the darkness and struck the active surface of this cell, where it was transformed instantly into a feeble electric current. Any object, no matter how thin, transparent, or small, would cause a registration on the cell if it cut through the beam.' This movement would indicate contact from the spirit world, although apparently there was no movement on the night of the secret experiment with the group of specially invited guests. However, this was said to be just one of Edison's devices spiritual inventions: he was also working on a 'Spirit Phone.' This Spirit Phone has never been found. Edison's prototypes and machines mysteriously vanished; or did they? In fact, Edison later denied he had ever been working on them!

In a 1926 New York Times interview, Edison said that his interview with B.C. Forbes in The American Magazine was just a prank. "I really had nothing to tell him, but I hated to disappoint him so I thought up this story about communicating with spirits, but it was all a joke." However, he had previously told the magazine, "I am engaged in the construction of one such apparatus now, and I hope to be able to finish it before very many months pass." Well, perhaps the mystery can be solved; fast forward now to one day in 2015, and French radio presenter Philippe Baudouin was browsing through a thrift store in Paris when he came across a very rare edition of Edison's diary. This 1949 French edition of Edison's original published diary was intact - with the final chapter that had been subsequently removed from later editions, and this chapter was dedicated to spiritualism and Edison's theory on communicating with those in the afterlife. It was a chapter that subsequent editions of his book had left out. This chapter also included Edison's plans for his elusive 'Spirit Phone', which he described in the chapter as an extremely sensitive phonograph apparatus which would be capable of picking up ghostly voices from the other side of the veil. These voices, he mused, were around us all the time, but this device would amplify them. The English version of his diary, which was widely circulated, had not contained this chapter. Baudouin re-published the original diary as 'Le Royaume de l'au-dela,' which translates as 'The Kingdom of the Afterlife,' in which Edison writes, 'I sought to build a scientific apparatus, allowing the dead, if possible, to enter into contact with us. If what we call "personality" remains after death, if the beings who have stripped the human form cannot act and move, they will communicate, at least with those they have left here below, thanks to my device which will give them this opportunity to "act."' Tom Woolworth from the organisation Itcvoices.org, who is an expert in Instrumental Trans Communication explains how the crucial chapter became lost. 'The Edison Estate not only redacted the 80+ pages of spiritualism from his diary and had it repressed, but the estate also held on to his documents for over 50 years until they were sent to Rutgers University. Only the first edition of this book has the section on Spiritualism. I have in my possession two "first" editions of this book by Edison. The very first publication run contains the information on spiritualism. After the book became public, his family called for the section to be redacted and a different "first" version was made available.'

Curiously, a séance was reportedly held 1941 in the presence of a medium called Mary Olson and other participants including Harry Gardner and James Gilbert Ernest Wright. Wright was a Scottish electrical engineer and researcher for General Electric. He'd invented putty and he was involved in the publication Borderland Sciences. He and Gardner claimed that during the séance,

Edison came through to them and told them all about the spirit machine he had been working on and where to find his lost blueprints and the prototype of the machine. Wright then claim they found the documents and built the machine, but they could not make it work. Regardless, they did go on to build their own machine, comprised of a small 'sound box,' a microphone and a loudspeaker. They claimed they were assisted in this by the spirit of Edison, who told them how to build it. Tim Woolworth says, 'The Edison estate has avowed that Thomas was never involved in work with a device to communicate with the dead because no plans, or instruments, have ever turned up.' For those who are interested, Itcvoices have the 'lost' chapter to read online, and in this chapter Edison wrote, 'This apparatus is in the nature of a valve, so to speak... it is similar to a modern power house, where man with his relatively puny one-eight horse-power, turns a valve which starts a 50,000 horse-power-steam turbine. My apparatus is along those lines... beyond that I don't care to say anything further regarding its nature. I have been working out the details for some time; indeed, a collaborator in this work died only the other day. In that he knew exactly what I am after in this work, I believe he ought to be the first to use it if he is able to do so.' Edison ends the chapter with, 'That is why I am now at work on the most sensitive apparatus I have ever undertaken to build....'

Another famous inventor, Scotsman John Logie Baird, born in 1888, and known as the inventor of the television, also recorded an interesting incident in his memoirs with regards to Thomas Edison. He begins it first with a fascinating tale; 'I was staying in a small hotel. One day, a bent up elderly man appeared in the board room. He was a professor and a distinguished entomologist and he had a very strange story to tell. It appeared he had been called in to investigate the activities of a medium called "Marjorie," a respectable married lady who had lost her only son in tragic circumstances. This boy "Jack" one morning in a fit of depression had gone into the bathroom and cut his throat, leaving the razor with bloodstained thumb marks on the floor; this razor had been locked away untouched.' Marjorie was heartbroken at losing her only son and she turned to a spiritualist circle to see if they could contact her dead son. Much to everyone's surprise, when she visited the circle, it was quickly discovered that Marjorie herself seemed to be in possession of remarkable mediumistic abilities. In the darkened room of the séance, she would go into a deep trance 'as her body extruded a strange vapour called ectoplasm. This extraordinary substance floated about her like a cloud and was of such a mysterious nature that it could be used by the spirits to build ectoplasmic bodies.' What happened next is extraordinary. 'The spirit of Jack her departed son appeared…Not only did he speak and answer questions, but he used the ectoplasm to materialise his hand and shook hands with the audience, wrote messages and moved objects and did all that a hand floating in space could do.' It was after this spectacular evening that the old etymology professor, who later approached Baird, was called upon to come to the spiritual circle to act 'as an independent scientific observer.' The Professor later told Baird that he 'approached the matter with complete scepticism and went to work with the careful thoroughness of a highly trained observer.' The elderly professor was hampered however by the fact that the seances always took place in the dark, as is customary practice for seances, 'with ectoplasm being highly sensitive to light which destroys it, with dreadful results to the medium, profuse bleeding and even death - such was the tale,' says Baird. 'Nevertheless, the professor shook hands with the ectoplasmic manifestation. The hand, he said, "Felt hard and cold like the skin of a serpent," but of its existence there was no doubt. Then he was struck with a really brilliant idea; no two thumb prints were alike, why not get Jack's ectoplasmic hand to make a fingerprint and compare it with the prints on the carefully preserved razor?' So, at the next séance, "Jack" was asked to press his ectoplasmic hand into a piece of wax, to leave his print. Then this print was compared with the prints on the bloody razor. 'The prints were identical,' says Baird; but it didn't end there. 'The professor had heard that I had a device which enabled a person to see in the dark. He wanted to borrow this so that he could watch the whole process of materialisation. I agreed at once to take part in this and he went off to arrange matters.' It was going to be tremendously exciting. However, it was not to be. 'I never saw him again. He was killed in a motor accident. A spiritualist told me that this was undoubtedly the action of the spirit forces and the result of his effort to pry into sacred secrets…'

It was shortly after this that Baird's contact with Edison came. It started with the arrival of a man at the company where Baird was working. The stranger had brought with him an invention that he wanted to show Baird. It was an electric motor controlled by a tuning fork. 'He had it with him but had some difficulty in making it run properly. I suggested he should come back when the troubles were overcome. He rose to go and as a parting shot said: "Would you care to have definite and irrefutable evidence of the survival of the personality after death?" I said, "Yes, I would give everything I possessed for such evidence." "Well," he said, "You only have to go to West Wimbledon". I duly arrived at the address given, a small highly respectable villa; here I was welcomed by a party of elderly ladies and gentlemen and given tea. Then a medium arrived, a nervous looking woman of about thirty-five. We trooped up to the séance room. Here there was arranged a circle of chairs and in the centre of this a small box like a sentry box, draped in black, with a chair. The medium was handcuffed to this chair. The audience sat round on the other chairs provided, each person held a hand of each of his neighbours and put a foot on one of his neighbour's feet, so that any undetected movement of hand or foot was impossible. Lights were then extinguished. The leader, an elderly gent with whiskers, then led the singing of a hymn. This was followed by a prayer. Then darkness and silence, broken only by a mysterious steady humming sound, which I learned afterwards came from an electrical tuning fork. The rhythmic sound was found to assist manifestations. We waited and waited, the darkness and silence had a most eerie effect, then the old lady next to me squeezed my hand and whispered "Look, it's coming." Sure enough in front of the booth, faint and almost invisible, a wavering purple coloured cloud was forming. It grew denser and then the silence was broken by the irregular tapping of a Morse key; the spirit was signalling by tapping in Morse code. The message was directed to me and it came from no less a person than Thomas Alva Edison. Edison had, it appeared, been experimenting with noctovision in his home in the astral plane, and he was convinced that it would in time prove of great use in assisting communication between the living and those who had passed over, but the time was not ripe and to attempt to use it now would incur grave danger. He was however continuing his research and would communicate with me when the time came to use noctovision.' Here Edison's message stopped and a new spirit took over, who gave her name as "Lilly." 'Lilly was more domestic in her messages and gave detailed advice to one of the circle upon what to do for her rheumatism and how to handle various family troubles.' It was at this point that Baird got up to leave. 'I remembered that I had a lunch appointment and time was passing, and so I whispered to the leader that I had an engagement and if he would excuse me, I would slip out. I bade a hurried and apologetic good-bye.'

CHAPTER THIRTEEN

'Father Gemelli was astonished to hear the voice of his dead father saying, "Of course I shall help you. I'm always with you."

In 1952, something quite stunning occurred in the Catholic Church in Italy. It involved two Priests, Father Ernetti and Father Genelli. Ernetti was one of the world's leading authorities on archaic music and he was passionate about physics and electronics. He had a degree in quantum physics and held a prestigious position at the Benedetto Marcello Conservatory in Venice. Father Ernetti was a former physician. One day, they were trying to record a Gregorian chant on a magnetophone, but the machine kept breaking. Father Gemelli became exasperated and asked aloud for his deceased father's help. To his surprise, his dead father's voice answered from the magnetophone. Later, when they were listening back to the recording, Father Gemelli was astonished to hear the voice of his dead father saying, "Of course I shall help you. I'm always with you. Zucchini, don't you know it is I? It is clear?" "Zucchini" was Father Gemelli's childhood nickname.

Father Gemelli and Father Ernetti were deeply troubled by this turn of events – for they knew that communication with the dead was regarded as forbidden by the Catholic Church, and in a quandary, they visited Pope Pius X11 for his advice. The Pope's consideration of the two priests' dilemma was surprising, for he told them that it was not so wrong. "You really need not worry about this. The existence of this voice is strictly a scientific fact and has nothing to do with spiritism," he told them. "The recorder is totally objective. It receives and records only sound waves from wherever they come. This may perhaps become the cornerstone for a building for scientific studies which will strengthen people's faith in a hereafter." The Pope's cousin, Reverend Dr. Gebhard Frei listened to the recordings and said, "All that I have heard forces me to believe that the voices come from individual entities." The recordings had captured more than just the voice of Gemelli's father – there were other spirit voices too. "Whether it suits me or not," said Frei, "I have no right to doubt the reality of the voices." After Reverend Frei himself died in 1967, his voice was also captured on a recording and those who knew him well confirmed it was him. The Vatican duly gave permission for its priests to conduct research into capturing these spirit voices, and Father Leo Schmid subsequently went on to collect over ten thousand recordings, which he collated in a book called When the Dead Speak, published in 1976. Four senior members of the Catholic hierarchy were involved in these recordings, along with Dr. Peter Bander. Dr Bander was a senior lecturer in Religious and Moral education at one of the colleges of the Cambridge Institute of Education. He was a trained psychologist and a Christian theologian, and initially he did not wish to become involved in this kind of research, but he was persuaded. The conclusion he came to was, "I heard a voice... I believed this to be the voice of my mother who had died three years earlier." Dr. Brendan McGann, who was Director of the Institute of Psychology in Dublin was also involved. He said, "Voices have appeared on a tape which did not come from any known sources." Father Pistone, who was also part of the project declared, "We recognize that the subject of EVP (electronic voice phenomenon) stirs the imagination even of those who have always maintained that there could never be any proof of basis for discussion on the question of the Afterlife. These experiments raise serious doubts even in the minds of atheists." Archbishop Cardinal Apostolic Nuncio was also part of the research team and he said, "Naturally it is all very mysterious, but we know the voices are there for all to hear." In 1997, Gino Concetti, chief theological commentator for the Vatican newspaper L'Osservatore Romano stated, "Communication is possible between those who live on this earth and those who live in a state of eternal response, in heaven. The

Church has decided not to forbid anymore the dialogue with the deceased." He quoted the dying Saint Dominic, telling his brothers, "Do not weep, for I shall be more useful to you after my death and I shall help you more effectively than during my life."

CHAPTER FOURTEEN

'The materialised people came out of the cabinet sometimes two or three at a time.... After a while, you forgot you were conversing with so-called dead people.'

Albert Best was born in 1917 in Belfast, Ireland. He was one of the most respected mediums of his time because of the extremely accurate evidence he gave during his demonstrations. He was a powerful healer too, though he shunned any publicity or attention. He was also the uncle of notorious footballer George Best. Albert spent much of his life in Glasgow, and in 1996, the Scottish Herald wrote, 'Too few people in Scotland and beyond knew his name, because he turned down repeated offers to appear on television shows.' The Newspaper then describes a remarkable incident that happened to Albert in his youth, which appears to show that he may have inherited his gift. 'He didn't know his mother or father. When he met his grandmother for the first and last time, she told him, "You'll be a widower before you're 24, and I'll be with you in Goubellet." He had no idea why he had received this message, nor what "Goubellet" meant.

In Belfast, Albert went on to marry a young local woman called Rose, and they had three children, but in 1940 after War broke out, he travelled to Algiers with the 6th Battalion, the Inniskillings. His troop's first job was to clear a grassy plain of enemy posts between two ridges. It was during this endeavour that Albert was shot by a nearby German soldier, and his body 'was dumped for burial with eight corpses.' However, as he lay there, a voice told him, "Get up!" So, he did, and, says The Herald, 'He walked away… to the terror of the Germans!' When Albert returned to his hometown of Belfast, he was greeted with the devastating news that his wife and children had been killed in an air raid. Albert had just turned 24; the exact age his grandmother had declared he would be widowed. But there was more; the grassy plain on which he'd been shot was called "Goubellet"; the name his grandmother had given him, when she told him she would be there, with him.

After the tragic loss of his wife and children, it was said that Albert could not bear to stay in Belfast; he was too heartbroken, and so he moved to Scotland, where he worked as a postman, 'until,' say The Herald, 'his success as a healer attracted the attention of a wealthy Scottish businessman.' The businessman generously funded Albert so that he could give-up his postman's job and spend all his time healing people, and Albert was able to open up a sanctuary outside of Glasgow. An article in Psychic News from 1972, as relayed by Belfast Spiritualist Church, has more information about his life. They say his mother died when he was just an infant and he was raised by a lady called Mrs Best, who he believed was his grandmother, though she wasn't. Then, at the age of 9, he suddenly became clairvoyant. 'Several times he "saw" an elderly man's spirit around the house. On one occasion when the spirit appeared, Mrs. Best spoke to it, and Albert heard her say, "Go away, father. You are frightening the boy." As he grew up, things got stranger when 'a psychic window-cleaner introduced the teenager to his local Spiritualist Church.' Albert began to attend and he sat in development for the next five years, 'constantly fighting what was obviously impending trance.' "It felt as though I had been chloroformed," said Albert, as a way of trying to explain what it felt like to go into trance. Then, at private home circles, 'he experienced memorable physical phenomena.' These included spirit materialisations. 'His spirit guides have materialised and shaken hands with him,' said The Herald. Even more astonishingly, 'Albert had the joy of holding in his arms the fully-materialised forms of Rose (his wife) and his three children.' It was Albert's evidential abilities for which he became most known publicly; though not widely, for he did not seek the limelight. The Herald describe the time he asked a visitor to the Spiritualist Church if he knew of a man called 'Wilson', and gave Wilson's address. The visitor had never been to the Spiritualist Church before, but it turned out that this was the address where his deceased brother had lived. Albert then asked the man if he was a boxer, adding, "Who is Rafferty? Did he break your nose?" The man admitted that this was indeed the case, although his nose did not show any obvious signs of the breakage. The man explained that he had got his broken nose at a boxing match from a man named Johnnie Rafferty.

Contemporary Scottish medium Gordon Smith also writes of a remarkable incident involving Albert in The Unbelievable Truth. Smith says that Reverend David Kennedy, a Church of Scotland minister, who would go on to write his own book A Venture in Immortality describing the incident too, was bereft at the death of his wife, and although seeking proof of life after death and contact with the departed was not in line with the Church, he set out to try to somehow hear from her again; for before her death, they had agreed that she would try to contact him from the afterlife. She would find a way, she told him, just before she died. The first medium he visited told him his wife's name was Ann and that she would contact him. "Your wife is determined... she will find a way." Reverend Kennedy went home, downcast. That wasn't good enough; and he despaired, apparently saying aloud, "Come on Ann, give me a sign, something that no-one could possibly know, please!" Smith describes what happened next; Kennedy lay down on the sofa, defeated. He was due to give a sermon later, and he had yet to even write it. Then, he must have fallen asleep, because the next thing he knew, he was woken by the sound of the telephone ringing. As he reached out to answer it, his eyes fell on the clock, which told him he had just five minutes until he was due to give his sermon! He ignored the phone and rushed around the room, trying to find a clean Vicar's collar to wear and simultaneously searching for any old notes he could use for the sermon; but the phone wouldn't stop ringing, and so in the end he picked the receiver up, hurriedly. "Your wife Ann is with me," said a voice. "She tells me that your clean collars are in the bottom drawer of your wardrobe. And the speech you prepared last year for this service is in the top drawer of your desk. Incidentally, my name is Albert Best." After the call ended, the Reverend did indeed find both his clean collars, and the pre-prepared sermon, exactly where he was told they would be. Best had told him that Ann also said he must send the 23 dirty collars to the laundry to be cleaned! When Kennedy counted the collars in the box that he was prone to throw them in, there were exactly 23 dirty ones in there. According to Smith, after this incident, whenever Reverend Kennedy sent out a thought to his dead wife, within a very short while Albert Best would be back on the phone with another message from her. In fact, on one occasion, Albert apparently phoned Kennedy and told him, "Tell your wife to stop bloomin' bothering me. It's the middle of the night!" When Smith himself was starting out as a medium, he was mentored by Albert and therefore he knew him very well. Smith writes, 'I remember Albert telling me he would often get annoyed with Ann's frequent requests for him to call her husband... Albert knew that she felt she had some kind of mission to convince her husband of her survival.' One day, Albert phoned Kennedy and told him to ask Ann's living sister about "ballet shoes." Ann's sister later explained that this referred to a private joke that had been known only between the two of them. What is lesser known about Albert Best was his astonishing spiritual healing abilities. His reputation often took him abroad to heal people, and on one occasion when he was in Africa, he is said to have met a witch doctor standing along a roadside. The witch doctor had set a small fire, and inside of it, the figures of Best's wife and three children fully materialised in front of his eyes. Albert's second wife recorded much of her husband's work in the book They walked among us. On one occasion, a seance was held in Cardiff and a guest who was present later described how, 'The materialised people came out of the cabinet sometimes two or three at a time.... About 20 fully materialised forms greeted us and spoke with us, quite naturally. After a while, you forgot you were conversing with so-called dead people.' Former editor of Psychic News, the late Maurice Barbanell, who had often watched Albert when he worked, stated, "The spirit forms not only show themselves in good red light, but they also hold sustained conversations after having walked about 10 feet from the cabinet." Rosalind Cattenach, in her book about Albert, Best of Both worlds: A tribute to a Great Medium, describes another occasion when a young man's life was dramatically assisted by Best's intervention; or rather, by spirit. A Mr. and Mrs. McDowell had gone to Albert's Spiritualist Church as a last resort. They would later say, "It was a super normal occurrence... an ordinary day perhaps for Albert but not for us." Their son John, had been seriously ill for a long time, and he had to go to hospital once a month. He was suffering from Giantism, and his condition was only getting worse. "There was no known cure at that time for our son," said his parents. The only option was radical surgery, which would give only a little respite from his condition, followed by a life-time on a strict drugs regime. On the day Mr. and Mrs. McDowell met Albert, they'd come directly from visiting their son in hospital. It was a Sunday and they had come to the Spiritualist Church in a last desperate call. They sat in the pews watching Albert giving a platform demonstration, when to their surprise he addressed them directly. "I have an Ernie Crangle here," he said. This was the name of Mrs

McDowell's deceased father. "He is saying to me that he knows the trouble you are having and his message is: "As King Canute had stilled the tide, the tide has been stemmed, worry no more. All will be well." Mr. and Mrs. McDowell left the Church puzzled and with no clue about what the cryptic message was supposed to mean. Two months passed by, and their son's condition remained unchanged and as serious as ever. In the New Year, the third month since their visit to the Spiritualist Church, they attended the hospital as usual with their son, for a range of tests. After the tests had been completed, a Doctor spoke with them. "One of the doctors questioned our son closely. He wanted to know what had happened in the interim," said Mrs. McDowell. The reason for this was that the condition of their son appeared to have stabilized. "It was a complete mystery to the medical team, and the doctor in the end admitted to our lad that "Something in the nature of a miracle had happened." The Doctors still continued to arrange for their son to have periodical tests, yet, each time, he received a clean bill of health. Twenty years later, and he was living a perfectly normal life; with no health problems whatsoever.

CHAPTER FIFTEEN

'The realisation dawned on him it had not been the medium he had greased but what it purported to be... a fully materialised spirit form.... The man looked up at me, his eyes wide, terrified.'

Dr. Douglas Baker was a medical adviser for the de la Warr Laboratories in Oxford, England in the 1960's. He was also very interested in spiritualism, including the possibility of spirit materialisation and he would go on to write Phenomena of Materialization in 1981. Dr. Baker believed his credentials of forty-plus years researching in this field would serve him well in his investigations, along with his qualifications as a medical doctor, and he said his life experiences, which included working as a wireless operator in tanks during the Second World War, and then in theatre production, made him somewhat 'qualified to undertake serious research into the matter of materialisation.' In order to be able to root out fraud, fakery and tricks, he believed it was helpful for investigators 'to have a scientific background and knowledge of human psychology and physiology as well as electronics.' For Dr. Baker, his journey into the mystifying world of spirit materialisation began when he kept coming across other doctors and surgeons during his medical training, who had already been to séances and 'discussed their experiences nonchalantly and openly.' All of them, he said, 'had participated in (rather than observed) materialisation.' As a result, they all 'held respect for the phenomenon that their expert hands had palpated and their trained eyes had seen.' In time, Dr. Baker would join their ranks by becoming completely convinced too, after seeing materialised spirits for himself.

Before Dr. Baker's conversion to true believer, he was on a lecture tour of South Africa when he was invited 'by a prominent surgeon in Johannesburg to attend a materialisation séance.' Baker makes clear that his attitude to such things at the time was; "It would not be true to say that I went to the séance to jeer… but when someone tells you that in full physical consciousness he saw forms materialise that were so firm beneath examining fingers as to be indistinguishable from ordinary flesh and bone … well, one is forgiven for being just the smallest degree sceptical. After all,' he adds, 'bone is a pretty firm tissue and could hardly assemble and disintegrate in a few seconds!' However, this was exactly what happened at a séance Dr. Baker attended with the English medium Alec

Harris. Dr. Baker explains that he searched Harris and the room thoroughly before the seance started. Harris was wearing simple black silk pyjamas. A black curtain was draped across one corner of the small room. The guests sat in two rows of chairs facing Harris. Six small red electric lights were lit around the room to allow visibility. Harris was seated less than 6 feet away from Dr. Baker. It was, says Baker, "Quite impossible for anything human to gain entrance to the corner except by being visible to all in the room." Everyone sang for about ten minutes to raise the positive energies in the room, then, 'a vague silver-white outline of a form appeared from the curtain.' Harris had not yet fully in gone into trance, and he appeared through the curtain, with 'the form of what appeared to be his dead sister.' The medium's wife Louie told everyone that the purpose of this was to prove that the two forms were separate entities. Next, 'A tall well-formed, human-like form parted the curtains and came close.' This spirit told the group he was Harris' control spirit. 'He was certainly an entity with its own personality and intelligence,' says Dr. Baker. Then, another spirit guide appeared who, 'Spoke to me personally... I held his hands and then felt all over the face, which seemed to be perfectly formed.' Baker says he noted carefully the 'warmth of the flesh and the firmness of the limbs. The pulse-beat seemed normal; veins, hair etc, all seemed to be present as with a normal human.' Then more spirits appeared. 'Sometimes, there were three or four forms in the room at the same time,' says Baker, adding, 'It was quite easy to see the medium sitting in trance when the curtains were opened wide.' In other words, the medium was not impersonating dead people. The figures that manifested, 'shuffled and made noises with their feet...If you can imagine yourself beneath water and a jellyfish floating up from the floor with its attending appendages tailing after it, and when reaching the surface suddenly turning into a human being, you will have a vague idea of how these forms arose from the floor in front of the medium.' How could this be trickery? How could this be people dressed up and impersonating spirits? And, when the figures left the room, they disappeared as such: 'The entity sank slowly (sometimes more rapidly) into the floor in front of the medium.' If this is so, then surely it was completely impossible for impersonators, dressing up as dead people, to have been tricking the group? Living people cannot simply vanish in front of your eyes by sinking into the floor; and they don't look like jellyfish either! As for the possibility of there being trap doors in the floor; if there had been people dressed up and masquerading as spirits, dropping down through a hole, then surely their body movements as they crouched and squeezed their body through, would have been visibly seen under the red lights by everyone? And, this is very different to literally evaporating into the floor, as Dr. Baker and other witnesses described it. The variety of spirits that appeared in human form included 'Children, a mother with a new born child, two red Indians, and men young and old, tall and short.' Baker estimates, 'There must have been more than 30 materialisations.' He saw ectoplasm too, describing that it can 'adopt the shape of any part of the human anatomy,' and, 'is not superficial but with arteries, ligaments, accepted anatomical shapes of various organs, like lungs, heart.' These spirits, he says, 'Evince the normal activity of such organs, manifesting a respiration rate, a heartbeat, a voice etc.' Ectoplasm has mass weight too, he says. 'When manifestations occur, the materialized form of say, a 6-foot man, when lifted, weighs about 10 or 15 lbs.' With regards to the problem of fakery, which as we know was quite common, Dr. Baker explains that in the seances he attended, 'The actual stages of "metamorphosis" that materialising forms go through – from a shadow-like structure, through an adumbration to a full materialisation – would be impossible to fabricate.' The red lights would have shown their "metamorphosis" happening, and Dr. Baker adds, 'Even more convincing, is when a form de-materializes in stages… a visible and palpable face that you are speaking to, which quite suddenly loses its lower jaw.' This, he feels quite reasonably, 'is hardly likely to be a fraudulent device.' The ectoplasm was coming from the nose and mouth of the medium, Dr. Baker observed, but he also discovered that it could emerge 'from the ears, armpits, naval, orifices in the lower trunk and even from the surface of the skin.' If ectoplasm is presented with white light, he says, it 'reacts strongly, and degenerates swiftly in its presence.'

In August 1960, Psychic News wrote an article about Dr. Baker's experiences. 'Baker reminds his readers he has been scientifically trained in the rationale of what a human body is composed of and how it works.' Again, it is explained how the spirits left the room; 'As quickly as these forms solidified from "nothingness," they disintegrated while they spoke.' The materialised spirits would quite literally loose shape and form and structure as they walked around the room, talking to the guests. Baker says that most of the guests were in bereavement and their deceased loved ones materialised, coming to see their family members, walking over to them and greeting them. A classics Professor, Dr. T. J. Haarhoff, who taught at the University of Wit-Watersrand in Johannesburg where Baker had studied for his medical degree, also attended some of the seances. Baker points out, 'Haarhoff's reputation was held in the highest esteem,' and the professor was apparently 'staggered when a materialised being spoke to him in ancient Greek,' which was, 'not only a language which Alec Harris knew nothing about, but also with a usage of words which could only have been known to students of ancient Greek.' Professor Haarhoff's conclusion was that the spirit materialisations produced by Alec Harris were, "Astounding, unique and entirely above suspicion…," and he added, "I make these statements after many years of investigating and many disappointments and experience of fraudulent mediums. One spirit walked out and took me firmly by the hand. He brought his face close to mine." As for Dr. Baker, he would use his stethoscope to test the spirits' breathing! He writes, 'I noted carefully the warmth of the flesh, the firmness of the limbs. The pulse beat seemed normal. Veins, hard prominences etc, all appeared to be present as with a normal human.'

We can learn more about Harris' seances from his wife Louie in her book. In March 1957, she and Alec emigrated to South Africa where their son and his wife lived, and during one of their private seances, Louie describes how her husband, while in trance, 'Stepped out of the cabinet and stood before us with ectoplasm streaming copiously from his solar plexus, mouth and nose… forming a large pool.' Then, 'After a few minutes, it started to build into a spirit figure.' There were more spirit appearances too; 'The old scientist who visited us,' a familiar spirit, 'bustles towards us, stocky of build, with an authoritative manner.' He tells the group, "Because we come in a body as solid as their own, they do not believe the evidence of their eyes. They cannot." Then he cautioned the group not to let disbelievers into the circle – because of the danger it would present to the medium. Louie says she took the scientist very seriously, because he only ever appeared when he had an important message for them. In fact, Mrs. Harris tried to cancel the next séance as a precaution. It was to be the last one before she and her husband took a much-needed break; however, her friend Vidie Carlton Jones urged her not to. Mrs. Jones had become an ardent believer in spiritualism after witnessing the physical return of her dead husband, a mining magnate who had materialised at one of Alec's previous séances. Mrs. Jones told Louie that new people were so eager to come to the upcoming seance, and she didn't want to let them down, and she stressed that she had "vetted" them very carefully. The new guests would be coming from the local Spiritualist Church, where the Secretary had booked two seats for himself and a fellow member of the Church, and Mrs. Jones insisted she could not tell them now that they could not come. Louie reluctantly agreed to proceed, but there was a twist; at the very last minute, the new guests asked Mrs. Jones if two other people could come in their place. Mrs. Jones readily agreed, thinking that they would be just as suitable for the séance, given that they also attended the Spiritualist Church. However, what Mrs. Jones did not know was that these new guests were actually journalists masquerading as spiritualists, and they were intent on uncovering what they believed to be a gigantic fraud being perpetrated at these so-called seances. So, the séance duly went ahead with everyone none the wiser. All the guests were seated in a circle and Alec was secured to a chair in the cabinet, with curtains hung in front of his chair. His spirit control soon appeared, who Louie describes as 'the slim bearded figure of Rohan.' He was 'standing uncertainly in the gap between the curtains.' This spirit was a regular visitor who always opened the séance, and he would routinely take time to talk to each of the sitters, 'taking his or her hands in his own slender ones.' On this particular night however, Rohan appeared reluctant to come out of the cabinet, and this perplexed Louie. When he did eventually venture out, Louie thought his manner suggested he was feeling very wary. Rohan made his way toward the circle of guests and began to greet them all one by one, then he returned to the cabinet and held up the curtain obscuring it, to give a full view of the medium strapped into the chair, to prove this was not Alec in disguise. Then he asked the group, "Can you see the medium clearly? Here I am, standing quite apart from him." Rohan then let the curtain fall back in front of Alec, and made his way to the back row of seats, whose occupants he had not yet got around to greeting. As Rohan reached the two undercover newspaper men who had been swopped in at the last minute, one of them launched into action. He 'sprang forward and grabbed him! Throwing his arms around the spirit figure, he held on to him tightly, shouting, "I've got you!" The newspaperman, says Louie, 'was obviously convinced he had captured the draped medium in the act of duplicity, masquerading as a spirit.' However, 'As Rohan's figure quickly dematerialised, there was a groan from Alec... then a cry of pain as the ectoplasm swiftly returned to his body with the impact of a sledge-hammer.' At the same time, 'the treacherous sitter fell dazed to the floor as the "solid" body he'd held so tightly minutes before disappeared.' Louie threw herself on top of the man, shouting at him, "You'll kill my husband!" Then she proceeded to flail at him furiously. The man underneath was understandably terrified; perhaps because Mrs. Harris was attacking him, but more likely, as Mrs. Harris herself puts it, 'The realisation dawned on him it had not been the medium he had greased but what it purported to be... a fully materialised spirit form.... The man looked up at me, his eyes wide, terrified.' As the ensuing fracas played out, the man's accomplice sprang from his seat to a nearby window, where he flung open the curtains, and immediately, camera flashes burst into the room. The two last-minute additions to the séance had brought along newspaper cameramen, and they'd been stationed outside, waiting to catch the supposedly fake medium in the act. As their flashes went off, blinding everyone in the room, the two reporters fled, swiftly chased by the angry group of sitters! Oddly though, when the photos were later developed, they were all completely blank. Unfortunately, Alec Harris was very ill after this incident, and his wife said it took him a long time to recover, although he never fully did. Having been so violently interrupted while he was in trance and profusely excreting ectoplasm from which the spirits were materializing, the substance had rushed back into his body at break-neck speed, causing significant internal distress to his organs.

The medium Douglas Johnson also gave his account to Psychic News in 1965, having attended an Alec séance in South Africa. He writes that his first surprise came, 'When a woman sitting next to him was kissed and held in the arms of her 'dead' doctor-husband.' Johnson himself shook hands with this spirit, and later said, "His handshake was warm and living." He also watched 'as the more than six-foot son of a Jewish couple materialised. He greeted, embraced and chatted to his parents.'

Zerdini, a former member of the spiritual research group The Noah's Ark Society, has provided more accounts of Alec's seances, and this next account comes from the rare booklet Materialisation, written by Harry Dawson, a former president of the National Spiritualists' Union. Dawson describes the time he attended one of Alec's séances with a couple of colleagues from the Union, including Ernest Thompson. 'During the proceedings, a little stocky figure came out of the cabinet, and stood by Ernest Thompson who was a heavy man, fourteen stone. This little stocky figure proceeded to lift Ernest right off the floor.' Dawson was a physiotherapist by profession, and he says that this made him intimately acquainted with how muscles in the body work. When the spirit appeared in the room, he became intrigued. 'I was so fascinated I went down on my knees in order to watch the play of the muscles in the calves of his legs.' While he was doing this, another member of his group entered the cabinet to ensure the medium was still seated in his chair – which, says Dawson, he was. 'The ectoplasmic form of the guide,' who Alec said was an Austrian scientist when he was alive, 'was visible to all of us.' There were three red lights on in the room, so that it was possible to see the spirit forms as they appeared. Dawson continues, 'As we watched, we saw ectoplasm begin to emerge slowly from the medium's mouth, nose and ears, it rolled down his body onto the floor where it coiled itself into a sizeable mass, and from the centre of this mass, it began to rise, just as if someone was pushing it upwards. It took the form of a little black boy.' The little spirit boy continued to materialize until he was fully-formed from the waist-up. 'The eyes, squat nose and teeth when it smiled was perfect.' When it was time for the little boy to leave, he 'began to dissolve before our eyes, and slowly like a thick black snake it climbed back over the body of the medium and was absorbed through the same orifices of the body.'

At a different séance, Dawson writes that a Mr. Ely, who was one of the guests, 'Immediately recognized his brother who passed as a result of wounds received in the 1914-18 War, for his brother had received an injury earlier in life which had disfigured the nose.' In other words, his brother materialized in the séance room and still had the same nose injury, which made him instantly recognisable in a plainly evidential way. Zerdini also provides another account. 'C. K. Shaw, asked the best form of mediumship for proving Survival, was most emphatic. "Materialisation," he replied, and recounted details of an Alec Harris seance.' Shaw says, "I was unknown to all present and had not expected anyone to materialize for me. My sister appeared. I looked into her face and eyes. It was my sister. I said, "Hello Maud, what are you doing here?" In Psychic News in 1962, another witness called Desmond Leslie, says, "I have been to a number of seances, good and bad. Perhaps the most impressive were those given by the Alec Harris circle in Cardiff where full materializations took place, sometimes two at once," and he continues, "The materialized beings could talk, sing and answer questions. One of them knew details of my life to which no-one in the room could have had access." As for the sceptics, Mr. Leslie says that the spirit figures "might for all the world have been a group of actors draped in cheesecloth; except that one of them dematerialized before our eyes." Perhaps even more astonishingly, Mr. Leslie adds that Alec himself disappeared. "For about twenty minutes, he existed somewhere without a physical body, thus proving for the first time the existence of a soul. Had he been only a body he would surely have been dead when he was put together again!" Another account, provided by Zerdini again, comes from Psychic News in 1965, where a séance guest called Donald Maclean later wrote, 'Curtains of the cabinet were drawn back to show Alec Harris in trance, with ectoplasm flowing from him. Out of this ectoplasm, on each side of him, a spirit child began to materialise.' The spirit children could be seen in the red lights of the séance room. They grew in size, then grew smaller again, 'as ectoplasm flowed to and from the medium.' Then another figure appeared, 'A healing guide,' says Maclean, 'who walked into the circle with a bright green-yellow sphere shining in front of him.'

Maurice Barbanell, a journalist and former editor of Two Worlds Magazine, also witnessed Harris on many occasions and he wrote, 'Thirty forms materialised during the two and a half hours.' Before this séance had got underway Barbanell says, 'I was asked to make a thorough examination of the room, of the cabinet, which was merely some curtains across one corner, and of the medium, who wore only a thin pair of trousers and a black vest.' When the spirits materialised, Barbanell was so close to the cabinet, 'that several of the forms had to walk over my feet.' Barbanell touched and handled 'the flowing ectoplasmic draperies' worn by the figures, and 'shook hands with two forms. Their hands were warm and normal.'

Zerdini has one more testimony about Alec. He says, "Here is the account of an outstanding seance written by a friend of mine, Reg Britten," from 1964. Britten writes, 'I attended six of his seances. This was under red lights bright enough to clearly see. When the curtains were drawn back, the sitters could all see Harris tied to his chair.' When the materialized spirits appeared in the séance room, they were 'every bit as solid as were the sitters.' Then his mother appeared. 'I was kissed on the lips by my mother's materialised form, I could distinctly feel her warm breath on my face.' Could he have been deluded, or deceived? Yet how could he mistake his own mother? And how could someone else impersonate his mother when he had never met anyone at the séance before his arrival? Other spirits appeared too he says. 'I had the opportunity of shaking hands with the forms. Their hands were warm and life-like. They gave as firm a grip as anyone in the room would have done.' When they left, 'They were frequently seen to dematerialise when the power was exhausted. This process often took place in the middle of the room and quite a distance from the cabinet… The form was seen to sink into the floor. The features would seem to melt and run as if they were wax before a fire.' This would certainly seem to make it impossible for the spirits to be living people dressed up as dead people. A living person cannot melt like wax! The spirit forms also sometimes 'built-up' in front of the sitter. 'I was able to watch the whole process of materialization,' he says. 'My attention was drawn to what appeared to be a dazzling white handkerchief on the floor in front of me.' Then, 'within seconds, this piece of ectoplasm rose quickly from the floor as if there was a stick under it pushing it up, although the whole time the material seemed to grow in height, so that the edge of the ectoplasm was always touching the floor. When it reached about four feet it could be seen to have a head on top of it, but a "dead" face with eyes closed and very pale.' Then, within the space of a few seconds, 'The face took on the appearance of a bronzed skin with an aquiline nose and high cheek bones.' During the seance, the cabinet curtains were opened and Alec was no longer there, tied to his chair. 'We were patiently awaiting the next form to build up and were watching the medium sitting slumped in his chair,' when the next moment, 'Our surprise was intense when we all realized that the medium's chair was empty. Nobody actually saw him vanish…. One moment we all saw him, and the next his chair was empty.' For approximately five minutes, Britten says, he kept his eyes fixed on the medium's chair. 'Then, we all saw what appeared to be a grey cloud form at the top of the cabinet. This cloud sank slowly downwards until it almost reached the chair, when it seemed to swirl around the chair. And there was Alec

Harris sitting in his chair, head sunk on his chest, and breathing heavily.' The sitters were dumbfounded, while Mrs. Harris simply remarked, "Now you know why we don't talk about this outside. They would say we were mad!"

CHAPTER SIXTEEN

'Her weight seemed scarcely as much as that of a child of eight years, but her arm felt solid upon my shoulder, and the lips that caressed me were as natural as life.'

Mrs. Elizabeth Bullock was an unusual spiritualist of the type called a 'transfiguration medium.' She lived in Manchester, England and Paul J. Gaunt, writing in Psypioneer Magazine, describes 'her rare and baffling form of mediumship.' Gaunt had personal experience of seeing it. 'I can remember some years ago, taking a well-known artist to a demonstration by Mrs Bullock,' he writes. The location was Edinburgh. The artist was Mr. John Duncan, RSA, who 'later describing his experience to some of his friends in a club in Edinburgh, said his dominating sensation was one of "fear."' At the séance, 'the artist studied the medium's face and head with the expert observation of a professional figure painter. He could have drawn her physiognomy from memory,' yet as the transfigurations began, 'he saw the contours of her head and face definitely change. He could not understand it.' Gaunt adds, 'Thousands of people have watched the extraordinary change in her features, any number of them have recognised the face taking on the familiar lineaments of some relative or friend.' Mrs. Bullock's face would literally change into those of the dead, who were related to people in her audiences, and they would be recognised as such. Famous faces also appeared, including W. E. Gladstone, the former British Prime Minister of England, and Nobel Prize winner George Bernard Shaw, the theatre playwright who penned Pygmalion. Mrs Bullock's introduction to spiritualism began when she turned to it after the loss of two of her children in infancy. In her grief, she began to attend Spiritualist Churches, and she joined a development circle. Her path was not without its difficulties however. Grant writes, 'She used to wake up in the night feeling that her head and face did not belong to her. She could even feel that her teeth had somehow moved and become different.'

Dr. Nandor Fodor, representing the Institute for Psychical Research wrote a report on Mrs Bullock after they'd studied her. 'Mrs. Bullock's face unquestionably changes,' he wrote, 'I saw things which I put down as impossible. I saw a moustache, a bear... yet I knew they were not real, as they could not be...I saw a shaft of shimmering light appear on her face and form into a transparent drooping moustache.' Fodor was intrigued and spell-bound, and he continued to study Mrs. Bullock. The first time he watched her, 'The lower part of her face became an amorphous mass, there was an ebb and flow over her face and new features were forming in place of her normal ones.' He'd invited Mrs. Bullock to the International Institute for Psychical Research to study her, where infra-red photos would be taken. As the tests got underway, many faces took over hers, including 'a Chinaman, a Japanese girl,' and a soldier 'with a circular wound in the forehead,' to which, 'exclamations of wonder' sprang from the mouths of the onlookers. 'It was a highly dramatic performance,' says Fodor, quite understandably. One of the people invited by the Institute to scrutinize her was a Mr. W. T. L. Becher, the managing director of Color Photographs ltd, who later said, "Changes began and the medium's face appeared to be plastic as if it were dough being kneaded by invisible hands," although he adds a curious suggestion, "Alternately, there may have been a rippling of the facial muscles under the skin, such as one notices under the skin of a tiger or cat about to pounce on prey…" There was also a physicist advising the study by the name of J.B. Hoper, MSC, who reported, 'The eyes, eyebrows, cheeks and chin changing simultaneously. The face appeared to be that of an old man, especially about the chin.'

Proof of the Afterlife

Raymond Buckland in his 1993 Book of Spirit Communication, mentions a Reverend J. Erwood who wrote about a 1931 séance with Mrs. Bullock, for the National Spiritualist Journal. This séance took place, 'In sufficient light to show every movement of the medium, who presented more than fifty faces within a period of an hour and a half.' Erwood observed, 'It was as though the medium's face were of plastic material being rapidly moulded from one form to another by some master worker in plastics.' Erwood said he saw, 'Oriental faces, Indians, calm, dignified, serious, spiritual,' in fact, 'almost every type of face was depicted during this most unusual séance.' What stunned Erwood the most though was when the features of a paralysed girl whom he had known when she was alive, appeared on Mrs. Bullock's face, and her body too. 'The medium's entire body, as well as face were twisted out of all semblance of its normal state, to depict the condition of this victim of paralysis.' Similarly, Alan Kardec, in his 1861 The Medium's Book, refers to a similar case that occurred in St Etienee, France, in 1858, which involved a 15-year-old girl who, 'had the singular faculty of transforming herself... that is to say, she could assume, at times, the appearance of persons who were dead.' He adds, 'So exact was the resemblance of features, expressions, voice, and even peculiarities of speech.' Most frequently, he says, the girl assumed the appearance of her brother, who had died many years earlier, 'Presenting the similitude not only of his face, but his height and the size of his body.' Kardec says a local doctor carried out an experiment, after having witnessed the phenomenon, in order to assure himself that this was not an illusion of some kind tricking him. 'It occurred to the physician to weigh this young lady, first in her normal state, and then in her state of transfiguration, when she had assumed the appearance of her brother.' Her brother, Kardec says, had been 'much larger and stronger than his sister.' Astonishingly, the result was, 'In the girl's transfigured state, her weight was almost doubled.'

Mrs Elizabeth J. Compton was a transfiguration medium too. She lived in New York State in the 1870's. She was part Native American and the mother of eight children. She was a washerwoman who could not read or write. She said that she first began seeing spirits at the age of nine. Former Colonel and Lawyer Henry Steel Olcott, an ardent spiritualist, wrote about her in his book People from the other World in 1875, after studying her closely. He said that her entire body would dematerialize. It was in March 1873 when her physical mediumship began to develop, rather inadvertedly. Apparently, Mrs. Compton's neighbour had called on her suggesting they should "form a circle" in the bedroom of another neighbour, Mr. Souls, who was lying sick in bed. Mrs. Compton at this point knew so little about spiritualist practices that, according to Olcott, she assumed her neighbour meant they should form a prayer circle, and she 'readily accepted.' So, the pair went to Mr. Soul's bedroom where they brought a table close to the bed, and sat down beside it. Almost immediately, Olcott says, 'She was astonished to hear rapping's under their hands.' It appears that the table was set up for the Ouija, because, 'a communication was spelled out, purporting to come from a young man named Melville Barton, who had been murdered a day or two before.' In fact, a search was currently in progress to try to find this man's body. The spirit, communicating through the table, 'described the murder, and indicated where his body would be found; which information the next day,' says Olcott, 'proved to be true.' After this, a year passed by until Mrs. Compton's husband 'proposed that they should try to get " materializations." The method he proposed was rather simple; 'A blanket was tacked over a door-way for the experiment.' What resulted however was not quite as rudimentary; 'Six spirit-hands were shown around the edges of the blanket.' News quickly spread about this, and, 'The experiment was repeated in many houses in Havana,' the results of which were 'uniformly satisfactory,' according to Olcott. At another experimental seance, 'Before long, the figure of a spirit-child appeared,' and, 'faces and busts of various persons.' As things progressed, 'the spirits began to talk in their own voices.' Apports came too; 'Flowers and other material objects.' Then, as the weeks passed by and

September came, 'A young girl calling herself "Katie Brink," an Indian warrior of the Seneca tribe, and a squaw named "Starlight" stepped out of the improvised cabinet, in full form.' In fact, that evening, a total of 6 spirits materialised, Olcott says. 'Katie Brink, the Seneca, Starlight, Katie Weaver, a Mrs. Rhodes and the Rev. Gardiner Crum.' It sounds more like a game of Cluedo! In order to ensure that all was above board, Colonel Olcott describes the lay-out of the séance room. 'Across one corner, a plastered partition has been run, forming a triangular cupboard, or closet, just large enough to admit of a person sitting in the apex of the triangle.' Inside the room, 'there is no window, trap or outlet, the walls being all solid, and the floor securely fastened down, with the boards running under the mop-board, except one which is badly matched; but this is nailed to the joists by a dozen nails and cannot be pried up without breaking it into pieces.' Usually there would be half a dozen or so spectators along with Olcott himself, all seated in chairs facing Mrs Compton, at a distance of about eight feet away. At one particular séance, Mrs Compton took her seat on the chair inside the small cabinet and, 'the lamp in the room was turned down very low, and for a long time nothing interesting occurred. Finally, the door opened and the figure of an Indian appeared on the threshold, spoke to us, greeted me cordially, but did not emerge, as he said the medium was in too weak and prostrated a condition to afford him the power.' At a séance the following evening, 'Katie Brink showed herself, and walked about, touching various persons, patting their heads and cheeks.' She approached Olcott, 'First gently stroking my head, she sat upon my knee, and passing an arm over my shoulder, kissed me upon my left cheek. Her weight seemed scarcely as much as that of a child of eight years, but her arm felt solid upon my shoulder, and the lips that caressed me were as natural as life.' As had been agreed before the séance began, Olcott was allowed to go into the cabinet then and examine the medium. To his astonishment, the medium was not there. The simple answer, of course, would have been that the medium was impersonating the spirit girl, and the spirit girl was actually the medium dressed differently. Olcott, unable to satisfy himself as to what was really happening, resolved to find out. The following evening, another séance took place with Mrs Compton, and Olcott describes some of the extreme steps taken before this séance began, in order to prevent any possibility of impersonation. Mrs Compton was restrained as such; 'She could not have been more firmly fixed to her seat if irons had been passed through her flesh, and riveted in the wood.' She was placed inside the cabinet and bound to the chair in a most unusual way. Thread was passed through the holes of her pierced ears, 'and sealing the ends to the back of the chair with sealing-wax, which I stamped with my private signet,' says Olcott.

He then secured her chair to the floor 'with thread and wax in a secure manner.' This was done in front of a number of named witnesses. If Mrs. Compton tried to get up now during the seance, the thread running through the holes in her ears would rip her ears in an excruciatingly painful way. There would also be physical evidence in the form of her injured and bloody ears, should she try to get up and move around. After this, the group of sitters, including Olcott, 'sang vigorously' for a while, until from above the door of the cabinet 'floated a pair of hands, from left to right and then disappeared.' Then, another pair of hands materialised, this time much larger. Then came a voice, addressing Olcott directly and instructing him on safety at the séance. Again, Olcott entered the cabinet to search it and to check on the medium, only to find that the medium had disappeared once more. Olcott left the cabinet and returned to his seat, to see a 'white robed' girl emerge from the cabinet. The spirit girl walked around the room and touched several of the people seated in chairs then, she 'compliantly stepped onto the weighing platform.' Olcott was going to weigh her with his Fairbanks platform-scale. The spirit girl weighed 77 lbs. Colonel Olcott rushed back into the cabinet again – but it was still empty. HE came back out and asked the spirit girl 'to make herself lighter if possible, and she stepped again upon my scales.' This time, the scales said 59 lbs! The spirit girl then walked around the room again, touching members of the group and finally 'sitting upon Mr. Hardy's knee, laying her hand gently upon my head, stroking my cheek, and then mounting the scale for me to make my final test. This time she weighed only 52 pounds, although from first to last there had been no apparent alteration in her dress or bulk.' Somehow, the spirit girl had changed weight in front of their very eyes; from 77 to 59 to 52 lbs! When she disappeared, a large male spirit appeared. He was an Indian Chief, who conversed with a member of the group called Mr. Hardy. 'A colloquy ensued in the Indian language between him and Mr. Hardy, who lived some years among the Western tribes, and who certified to the reality of the speech uttered by the spectre chief.' Olcott reasons that the materialisation of this male spirit, who upon leaving gave a "whoop-whoop" call which reached the rafters with its deep vibration, 'would seem to indicate that the poor, nervously fluttering medium had no part in the appearance of at least this one spectre.' When this figure vanished, the group turned up the light and, 'various faces floated into sight above the door and faded away.' At the end of all this, Olcott went back into the cabinet carrying a lamp, and he found the medium in her chair, 'just as I left her at the beginning of the séance, thread unbroken and every seal undisturbed!' Her ears were not torn to shreds; she had not left her chair for the entirety of the séance. However, Mrs. Compton 'sat there with her head leaning against the wall,' and she was not in a good state. 'Her flesh as pale as marble, her eyeballs turned up beneath the lids, her forehead covered with a death-like damp,' and, 'no breath coming from her lungs, no pulse at her wrist.' Before they attempted to revive her however, Olcott says, 'Every person examined the threads and seals,' and only then did Olcott cut the medium free! He 'carried the woman out, and she lay thus inanimate for eighteen minutes, life gradually coming back into her body until respiration and pulse and the temperature of her skin became normal.' Now revived, Olcott took her to the weighing platform. She weighed 121 lbs. The spirit girl had weighed 77 lbs, then 59, then 52 – nothing like the weight of Mrs Compton! And what had happened to make the spirit weigh different amounts each time?

Sir Arthur Conan Doyle, on learning about the incident, asked, "What are we to make of such a result? The facts seem to be beyond dispute." There were 11 other people present alongside Olcott who all witnessed the same thing. "What are we to deduce from such facts?" Doyle asks. "If the ectoplasmic figure weighed only 77 lbs and the medium 121 lbs, then it is clear that only 44 lbs of her were left when the phantom was out." He continues with his hypothesis, "If 44 lbs were not enough to continue the process of life - may not her guardians have used their subtle occult chemistry in order to dematerialise her and so save her from danger 'til the return of the phantom would enable her to reassemble?" He concludes, 'It is a strange supposition, but it seems to meet the facts.' Colonel Olcott's conclusion about the seances was, 'This was indeed being face to face with the dead, or rather, with the quick who had tasted death, and passed on into an immortal life where death is known no more.'

CHAPTER SEVENTEEN

'Mrs. Houseman said in a matter of fact voice, that she had been cured of a crippling affliction by a surgeon who had returned from the dead to operate on her.'

JJ Thomas, known as 'Jessie', was a medium and healer who had 'thousands of successes to his credit,' according to the National Spiritualist Union, who wrote a retrospective on Thomas in their Pioneer journal in August 2016. Thomas discovered he was different to other children as a boy of just 6 years of age. As an adult, he would go on to become a 'psychic surgeon.' The SNU says, 'Thomas specialised in healing by psychic "operations". His guide went through all the motions of a surgeon performing an operation… some of them even confirmed by medical men,' but it all began when was just 6 years old. 'On three successive nights his father, a ship's engineer away at sea, came to his bedside and said, "Go tell your mother I am dead." Young Jessie duly told his mother, but naturally, she chided him. 'Later however, confirmation came that his father had in fact died on the first night of his appearance.' As Jessie grew to adulthood, he worked as a mechanic by day in his home town of Brighton, England. By night, he sat in a development circle, where spirits began to come through to him as he went into trance. Before World War II broke out, he'd opened a healing centre 'in a bare room over his garage.' When the War came, he joined the RAF to fight for his country. When peace broke out, he returned to Brighton where he resumed his healing work. Medical professionals in the spirit world had started to come through Jessie, to treat the members of the public who came to see him, and rather astonishingly, the National Spiritualists' Union says, 'Among his healing guides was one recognised by some patients as a former doctor whose practice was in the East End of London.' Jessie's chief guide however was a "Doctor Robert," 'who carried out '"operations" on the etheric bodies of sick patients.' This doctor would later be identified as Professor Robert Koch, who had been born in Germany in 1843. According to Dr. Koch's parents, he had taught himself to read by the age of five. As he grew up, he went on to study medicine at University in Germany. He volunteered for service in the Franco-Prussian War, and after the war, he returned home, where anthrax had become a major problem to the farm animals surrounding his town in the Wollstein district. With his medical background, Dr. Koch became determined to study the disease, to see if he could do anything to stop the animals suffering, even though he had no access to a laboratory there. Quite remarkably, he succeeded in developing new methods of studying bacteria, which he continued to do when he moved to Berlin, where he also began to study tuberculosis. He travelled to Egypt to help with a cholera outbreak, and while there he discovered the cause of the disease. Back in Berlin, he became Director of the new Institute for Infectious Diseases, and he travelled to both Africa and India to assist with terrible infectious outbreaks there too, including malaria and typhus. In time, he discovered the causative organisms of anthrax, septicæmia, tuberculosis and cholera. For his outstanding breakthroughs, he was awarded the Nobel Prize 'for Physiology or Medicine' in 1905. Then, over a century later, Dr. Koch made a comeback! His spirit began working through Jessie Thomas, and Jessie made a visit to Hamburg, where he gave a healing demonstration to a panel of doctors, who, 'though they stated that his diagnoses were 100% accurate, the health authorities refused to give him permission to do healing.' The patients that Jessie diagnosed in front of the doctors were people he had never met before. His experience in Hamburg was one that many healing mediums would experience across the world through the ages. In Jessie's case, verified accounts of his healing work exist, such as those reported in the May 1953 edition of Two Worlds magazine, and they are simply astounding. A Mrs Madeline Horseman, aged 60, said she had received healing from Jessie and his spirit healer, Dr. Robert. Mrs Horseman was a laundry manageress from Salisbury, who told Peter Small, the reporter for Two Worlds, 'in a matter of fact voice, that she had been cured of a crippling affliction by a surgeon who had returned from the dead to operate on her.' Mrs. Houseman, 'was a sensible housewife and business woman, inclined neither to sensation nor superstition. Her story was that four years prior, she had been diagnosed with a dropped abdomen.' She was pronounced "incurable," and the only treatment for the condition was to wear a heavy girdle made of steel, after having already endured three operations for the condition, to no avail. After her healing session with Jessie Thomas however, 'She was apparently a perfectly fit woman. Her relatives and colleagues in Salisbury confirm this.' Mrs. Houseman was as shocked as anyone – she'd been a complete sceptic on matters spiritual. She said, "I first went to see Mr. Thomas because my family dared me to. I was never a spiritualist and didn't believe in that sort of thing, but I'd worn an uncomfortable belt and after three operations doctors said they could do no more." Mrs. Houseman had come with her family to the seaside town of Brighton for a holiday, and this was when her family had dared her to visit Jessie. "He operated on me, but it didn't seem to have any effect," she said. Two days later however, she felt very unwell. Jessie had warned her that this might happen. A few more days then passed by, after which she said, "The remarkable thing happened. I felt as if a great weight had been lifted from me." Feeling curious about this new sensation, she removed the heavy steel girdle from around her stomach, only to discover, "My stomach was once again a normal size!" That was four years ago, she said, "And I haven't worn a belt or had any pain since that day." Mrs. Houseman's brother told the reporter, "Even now, I can't make top nor tail of it… if it weren't my own sister, I wouldn't believe it." Mrs. Houseman's manager at the Laundry also confirmed Mrs. Houseman's physical transformation; from being riddled with crippling pain to becoming pain-free and completely healed.

The "operating" room in Brighton where Mrs. Housemen had received her treatment, said the reporter, was nothing like a surgery. It was just a sparse, mostly-empty room, 'with a couch for the patient to lay on, which would serve as the operating table.' When Jessie was being interviewed, he told the reporter, "Dr. Robert is the spirit who uses my body. He was one of the leading surgeons in Germany until he died 66 years ago." Jessie said he could talk with the doctor 'in an ordinary manner,' just like talking to you or I, until he begins to work on the patient and then he goes into trance. "Dr. Robert takes over my body completely." The reporter describes how the healing was performed; Jessie, dressed in a white overall over his clothes, said a short prayer, closed his eyes and breathed deeply for a few moments, with his wife in the room acting as the assistant. As the "operation" then got under way, the spirit Doctor, using Jessie's hands, 'went through the motions of incisions, stitching up, and so on.' Jessie told Small that the operation was performed on the patient's 'spiritual body,' and that it could take a couple of days for the operation to take effect on their physical body. Dr. Robert, speaking through Jessie, says, "As I can see right into the body, I can get right to the source of the trouble without bothering about the area of pain." The spirit doctor explains his ability to distinguish between healthy organs and those with disease. He says, "Diseased organs are grey, and healthy ones, red surrounded by blue." Jessie carried out 'absent healing' too, with Dr. Robert working on the patient in their sleep.

Well, if this all sounds too bizarre to be believed, it gets stranger, because after Jessie died, it would appear that Dr. Koch continued his "spirit operations" by working through another medium called Tom Pilgrim. Pilgrim had visited Jessie when he was suffering from a stomach ulcer. Pilgrim had been receiving treatment for the ulcer from his own doctor, but the treatment was not working. Long before this however, and without Pilgrim being aware that the spirit doctor was working through Jessie, or even knowing who Jessie was, Dr. Koch had apparently already made his presence known to Tom Pilgrim. Pilgrim explains this in his autobiography, which was published in 1982 when he was still alive. He says that early one morning in 1946, he was walking along a street in his home town of Brighton. He noticed that even though it was early, there would usually still be lots of cars and people about, but this morning, 'it was strangely quiet.' Then, all of a sudden, he heard a voice call his name. He was surprised, as he did not live near this street and was on a visit to the locality for his job. He stopped walking and looked all around, but he couldn't see anyone calling him. 'I carried on, feeling a little uneasy,' he says. Then he heard the voice once more, only louder this time. He stopped again, and looked up at all the windows in the houses in the street, trying to find someone calling him from a window. The voice was louder this time, but he still couldn't see anyone who could be responsible for it. However, 'High above the houses, outlined against a clear blue sky, I saw a huge cross, the colour of burnished gold.' He rubbed his eyes, but when he opened them again it was still there. 'It was exquisite! It stood in the motionless air as if sculpted; so solid you thought you could climb up it.' Eventually, the cross began to fade away. He couldn't understand it. Although it was incredibly beautiful; he wasn't a religious man. He was very puzzled, and in search of an answer he took himself off to the local Church, where he sat in a pew every night for 7 nights, hoping the answer would present itself to him there; but

Proof of the Afterlife

nothing happened. Finally, he sought out the Church vicar and explained what had happened to him. The vicar did not have an answer for him either. Three months passed by, and Pilgrim was lying in bed one night reading a book, when suddenly he looked up and saw a man standing in his room. 'I wanted to ask a thousand questions of this man at the foot of my bed, but I couldn't bring out a single word.' The man looked at him in silence and then slowly disappeared. Two more months passed by, and the man appeared once more, only this time he spoke. 'He had been a doctor in his earth life, he told me, was continuing his work in the spirit world, and would like to use me as his medium when the time was ripe. He gave his name as Dr. Robert Koch, and aware of the fact that I couldn't understand his surname, spelled it out for me.' Even still, says Pilgrim, 'his surname foxed me, so I decided to call him simply Dr. Robert.' Pilgrim had already been practising healing for some time when this happened, but now, as he gave healing to people who came to him in need, he would often see the spirit doctor in the room with him.

It was not long after this that Pilgrim, unable to bear the pain and discomfort of his own ulcer, decided to pay a visit to the medium and healer Jessie Thomas, who he had now come to hear about, but had no idea that Jessie worked with Dr. Koch too! All Pilgrim knew was that Jessie had a reputation for being an excellent healer. So, off he went to see Jessie, hoping to get some respite from the pain. As Jessie ushered him into the sparse treatment room above the garage, 'Jessie went into a deep trance, and the spirit entity who came through to treat me was none other than Dr. Robert!' Then, rather comically, he 'thumped my tummy and said, "I'm going to take this ulcer out. It will take twenty minutes. Do you want to talk?" Pilgrim replied that he did, and the spirit doctor proceeded to describe Pilgrim's life from childhood to present. "We know more about you than you know yourself," Dr. Robert told him. "Tomorrow you may have pain - don't regret having come here... the pain will become less each day and at the end of the week you'll be cured. I'm leaving now." Pilgrim goes on to explain more about these spirit operations. He says they are performed 'on the etheric counterpart of the physical body; they take place in a different dimension, and so you never feel any pain when the actual operation is carried out; but the results are transferred to the physical body, which has to 'catch-up' as it were, and that is a process you may feel.' After the spirit doctor left and Jessie came out of trance, Jessie said to Pilgrim, "You are going to do this work yourself one day." When Pilgrim went to see his own doctor and X-rays were carried out, the results showed that his ulcer had entirely disappeared. Pilgrim was astonished. So too was his doctor. "It was a large, serious ulcer! How come it is no longer there?" his doctor asked, completely puzzled. Pilgrim told the doctor what had happened, to which the doctor, fortunately being an open-minded man, said, "Good for you!" Dr. Robert's prediction also came true. 'Round about 1960, after JJ Thomas had passed on, I became Dr. Robert's medium.' However, Pilgrim still didn't really know anything about the spirit doctor, other than his name. Then, fast forward to 1979, when a journalist was interviewing him. Pilgrim mentioned the spirit doctor, and the journalist, understandably curious, asked why Pilgrim didn't use the doctor's surname. Pilgrim explained that he found it difficult to use because he wasn't sure how it should be pronounced. Of course, in those days there was no internet to help Pilgrim. He tried to pronounce "Dr. Koch", to demonstrate to the journalist, and she exclaimed, "There was a famous German doctor and scientist of that name, who received the Nobel prize for medicine early this century!" This meant nothing to Pilgrim, who says, 'I didn't have a clue.' However, as they sat talking, suddenly he saw the spirit doctor in the room with them, 'with a highly amused expression on his face.' Pilgrim turned to the journalist and told her that the doctor was in the room now and was telling him that he was willing to answer any questions she might have. Dr. Koch told Pilgrim that he had been born in what sounded to Pilgrim to be 'Clausweil,' or 'Clauswal.' He said he had been born in 1843, and had become a doctor of medicine in 1866. He explained that he had served in the Franco-Russian war as a medical officer, had discovered the tuberculosis bacillus in 1882 and had received the Nobel Prize for medicine in 1905. He said he had died in Baden-Baden in 1910. Pilgrim wrote all this down as the doctor spoke to him, and handed his notes to the journalist. The following day, Pilgrim received a telephone call from the journalist, who told him she had done some research. "I compared the notes you wrote down with those relating to Dr. Robert Koch in a German encyclopaedia. They are correct, and his birthplace is given as "Clausthal". Your Doctor Robert really is the famous German scientist Dr. Robert Koch!" Pilgrim says that this revelation left him feeling rather overwhelmed. Tom Pilgrim passed away in 2002 at the age of 92. In his lifetime he would receive up to 200 letters a week with requests from the general public for healing. In his autobiography, Pilgrim's early life and journey into mediumship is described in more detail. One day at school, he was told at the last minute to fill in for the football team goal keeper. This filled him with dread, as he had never played in the team or been a goal keeper before. He was 10 years old at the time. As the game got underway, Pilgrim felt himself relaxing a little, and soon he became distracted by a group of younger children who kept running on and off the pitch, chasing each other. He knew no-one else could see them. Unfortunately, the children distracted Pilgrim so much that he didn't see the

Proof of the Afterlife

football come hurtling toward him and the goal, and he failed to stop the ball going in. The next day at school assembly, he was publicly shamed by the head master, who told the whole school it was Pilgrim who had made them lose the match – to a bottom of the league team too! This was not the first time Pilgrim was in trouble at school – and it was all because he could hear and see things that the other couldn't and they were always distracting him. He told everyone what he could see or hear; he wanted to share it, but no-one believed him and he would end up getting punished for it. He insisted he was telling the truth; but it was no use. His school form master was particularly scathing. "All right, Pilgrim, go on, tell the class about your invisible friends," he would say, laughing, and the whole class would join in the ridicule. Young Pilgrim would tell his mother, who did understand, because she was a medium herself. Her father too, a blacksmith, had been a clairvoyant. Pilgrim's family were ordinary, working-class people. His father was a postman and his mother worked as a cook and cleaner for wealthy local families. She couldn't work as a medium because the Witchcraft Act of 1735 was still in place at this time and if she became known as a medium, she could face imprisonment. However, she did invite friends to tea-parties, where she would read the tea leaves for them. She didn't need to use the tea leaves; they were just a devise to disguise her clairvoyance and save her from possible prosecution. After leaving school, Pilgrim's first job was at a leather workshop where they made suitcases and other bags. Four years later, he looked for something more interesting and secured a job at a photography company where he learned how to develop pictures. During his time off, he volunteered with the town's poorest people, accompanying them to apply for financial help from institutions. During the Burma War Campaign, he was based in South Africa with the Royal Air Force. The RAF planes were flying in bombing raids. Pilgrim was part of the salvage unit, sent out to find downed planes and their crew. 'We usually found the crashed plane, the decapitated bodies of crews lying nearby, sometimes horribly mutilated.' Quite naturally, this made Pilgrim ill at the sight of it. When letters from his wife and child back home stopped coming, Pilgrim had a mental breakdown. His eardrums too had been perforated and he was in excruciating pain. 'I went berserk,' he says, 'and three blokes had to sit on me to keep me down.' Eventually, he was sent to Calcutta to recuperate and in time, he was given a medical discharge. When he finally got home to Brighton, his wife confessed that she had been unfaithful to him, twice, and had got pregnant by a Canadian service man who had now left with his unit. The baby had died a few days after childbirth, she said. The only positive thing Pilgrim had going for him at this time was that he was given his old job back at the Cooperative where he worked as storekeeper of the pharmacy department. While at work, he would come across colleagues or customers who had ailments and gently he would offer healing to them from a room in his house; but it wasn't until he saw that huge solid golden cross in the sky and heard his name being called, that he met Dr. Robert Koch, who had appeared in his bedroom one night, and after being healed himself by Dr. Koch, Pilgrim's healing took on another level.

A patient called Ivan Brown, 'a giant of a man,' had been a keen sportsman until a fall injured his back. By the time he visited Pilgrim, he had been forced to give up his job as a painter and decorator, and was living 'in daily agony.' Frequent visits to the hospital for treatment rendered no respite from the pain. They told him he'd have to live with it. Upon arriving at Pilgrim's home, he shuffled in, explaining that he'd only come because his wife had begged him to. As the healing session got underway, Pilgrim says, 'I became conscious of Dr. Robert concentrating on one particular spot on the patient's spine. I felt my fingertips digging in hard and pushing at something – once, twice.' Then Pilgrim heard Dr. Robert say, "That's it, that's it. He's cured." Mr. Brown returned immediately to work, resumed his sports, and was able to rough and tumble with his young children again – activities he could never have imagined being possible. As word spread of Pilgrim's successful healings, patients were soon travelling from far afield to see him. "People from the continent drive out to me straight from Heathrow and after healing, straight back to Heathrow to catch a plane home." Pilgrim made no charge for his healings and if a donation was made, he would give a large portion of it to charity. Dr. Robert told Pilgrim he would help anyone who was suffering, 'but he is a man who doesn't suffer fools gladly. He also told me that we do not change our basic character when we leave earth life,' and, 'with all the selfless service Dr. Robert gives to humanity, he still retains his basic traits; like any other human being in this world or the next, he can feel happy, or sad, elated, frustrated or hurt; he can get impatient, excited, angry, and rarely – very cross indeed.' On one occasion, an elderly lady arrived for healing at Pilgrim's home in a very bad mood. "I'm no better than when I came to you last time," she told Pilgrim. Patients who came for healing very seldom received an instantaneous cure – they would usually need to come for several sessions, Pilgrim explains. The old lady who came back was suffering with terrible arthritis, and after having a go at Pilgrim she then proceeded to walk up to the portrait of Dr. Robert hanging on the wall, and wagged her finger at him accusingly. "And it's about time you did something as well!" she told the painting. 'Dr. Robert,' says Pilgrim, 'who stood near the door with eyebrows raised and arms folded across his chest, took one look at the lady as she stood finger-wagging before his portrait, gave a snort of disgust, turned on his heels and left.' This left Pilgrim in a quandary. 'There I stood with no spirit doctor and a waiting room full of patients.' He had to tell the old lady, "I'm sorry but I don't think I can help you." Fortunately for Pilgrim, when the next patient came in, Dr. Robert was back. 'He still looked angry,' says Pilgrim, but he gave a reassuring smile. "You didn't think I'd leave you?" asked Dr. Robert. In fact, Pilgrim explains that the spirit doctor did not always work alone. Other doctors would sometimes come and join him to work on a patient. They included 'Richard Gouldon, a famous eye-surgeon who used to work at the Royal Free Hospital during his earth life,' and 'another German physician, Dr. Heinenmann,' as well as a Chinese doctor, 'known to me simply as "Chang." Pilgrim adds, 'I have on occasion seen all the members of Dr. Robert's group gathered around a hospital bed when I'm treating an in-patient.' At least one of Pilgrim's patients saw Dr. Koch too; a Mr. John Hickey had come to see Pilgrim with a twisted septum in his nose. The hospital had told him he would need to have his nose broken and the septum straightened, or they could give him a plastic nose. Neither option appealed to Hickey, quite understandably, and he visited Pilgrim to see if there was anything he could do. On the train journey home, Hickey dozed off for a while, until waking suddenly to find a man standing over him. Still half-asleep, he couldn't understand why the man appeared to be wearing very old-fashioned clothing. Later, he recalled that Pilgrim had told him of a spirit doctor who worked through him. "I realized this man in old-fashioned clothes was none other than Dr. Robert. There he was – so real – so solid." Pilgrim says that Mr. Hickey was quite correct, because when Pilgrim later asked Dr. Robert if he had been on the train, the spirit doctor replied that he had indeed been checking that all was in order with the patient's nose. "He woke just as I was bending over him," Dr. Robert told Pilgrim, who adds that the doctor was usually careful not to show himself to patients since a female patient had once woken woke in the middle of the night screaming in abject terror after seeing Dr. Robert as he was giving her absent healing! 'He was very indignant at what he considered her illogical reaction," says Pilgrim. Dr. Robert was most offended by her reaction. "What was she afraid of?" he reasoned, "Seeing me should have been confirmation that I really do exist." Although Tom Pilgrim passed away in 2002, the story doesn't end there. Steven Upton is a former tutor at the Arthur Findlay College of Spiritualism and psychic sciences. Perhaps coincidentally, Steven was also in the Royal Air Force, just like Tom Pilgrim before him, and healer Jessie Thomas before Pilgrim. When Steven visited me one day in June 2022, he told me about this; but the similarities between these three mediums don't stop there. Steven told me that one day he was giving a trance

Proof of the Afterlife

healing demonstration to a class he was teaching at the Arthur Findlay College. This is a world famous residential psychic science college where mediums from beginners to advanced take classes to further develop their abilities. In this particular class, one of the students was a psychic artist, and as Steven gave his demonstration, she found herself sketching the portrait of a man she could see standing on the platform behind him. The man wasn't physically there, but she could see him clairvoyantly. At the same time, though neither Steven nor the psychic artist knew it, another student in the class, who used to be a nurse, also clairvoyantly saw a man standing behind him. Shortly after this, the former nurse found herself going to a medical library to look through the books. She felt sure she had seen this spirit man before somewhere and she felt that he had something to do with medicine. As she flicked through the books she felt drawn to, she came across the photograph of a man who looked exactly like the spirit man she had seen standing on the platform. She took the book to show Steven, who had no idea about a man standing behind him, but the strange thing was, the sketch the other student had drawn in his class was identical to the man in the photograph in the book. The man's name was Dr. Robert Koch! This still meant nothing to the Steven – he told me he had not been aware of any spirits standing behind him in the class, nor when he gave healing to individual patients. Perhaps it was all a strange coincidence then; but after this had happened, Steven told me that he was giving another demonstration at a different location and when the class finished, a man in the audience approached him and asked him if he knew a man called "Tom Pilgrim." Pilgrim, as we know, used to work with the spirit doctor Robert Koch, as did JJ Thomas before Pilgrim. So, it would seem that the spirit doctor now works through Steven Upton, who is both a medium and a trance healer. In Steven's case, he tells me that he was not aware of the Doctor's presence. When he gives healing, he explains, he goes into deep trance and into what is almost like a void – a state of blankness that is not easily achieved but which lets the spirit doctor and any other helpers in spirit world have unfettered access to the patient to work on them unhindered by the mind of the healer. Steven 'gets out of the way,' like most healers; in other words, they purposely do not try to sense or see what is happening during the healing session, in order that their energies do not interfere with the spirits working on the patients. This is not unusual, having spoken with many healers; in fact, it's the most effective way to deliver healing, and to some extent even essential in order to allow the spirits to do their work without interference. My close friend who is also a mediumistic healer of many decades, also works in this way, where he sees and feels very little during the healing sessions, and this is also the case for healers I have spent time with at the Harry Edwards Healing Sanctuary. The common consensus is that a healer must "get out of the way," let go, and let the spirits work. Healers do not attempt to "link" with spirits clairvoyantly and do not usually communicate with them when they are healing.

Not all spiritual healers have spirits doctors working through them. In fact, it's exceptionally rare; or rather perhaps, it is very unusual for mediums to see and hear and talk to spirit doctors when they are carrying out healing, although that doesn't mean of course that spirit doctors aren't working with them; its just that they aren't necessarily making their presence known to the medium. What is certain is that mediums who are "psychic surgeons," who have spirit doctors carrying out "operations" on patients is still incredibly rare. Steven Upton, a world-class trance healer, has described some of the cases where people have come to him for healing. For example, a lady once came to him with scars on the retina of one of her eyes. Her vision in that eye was only about 30%. Doctors and surgeons had told her that it was impossible to get rid of the scarring. Steven went into trance and gave her healing, with a doctor present to act as a witness. Subsequently, when the lady returned to the hospital for tests, the scarring had simply vanished. In another instance, a lady had come to see him and she was also suffering with vision problems. He told journalist Sharon Blauer, "During the session, no healing energy went to her eyes at all – they went instead into the emotional system, causing a powerful release. I became aware that around 20 years earlier, she went through a traumatic incident in her life that had blighted her life ever since." The spirits, working through Steven, had focussed on healing this trauma for her first– rather than her eyes, and then she returned for a second session (healings are not usually instantaneous). In her second session, her eyes were healed so that her vision became perfect. Afterwards, the lady explained that over two decades earlier, she had married on a Friday and been widowed by Sunday. Ever since then, she had not entered into a relationship again, because she had been too traumatised, but, "On the evening of the first sitting, at home she saw her husband: clearly and objectively." In another case, a Dutch woman who was attending the Arthur Findlay College where Steven was teaching, had difficulties with her feet. They had been growing outwards for years. "Her left foot was twice the size of the right. She wore trainers that were slit open to get on her foot. Doctors had said her condition was incurable." Steven gave her spiritual healing, and within a few days, "She showed me her feet again. They were completely normal. Fifteen years of bone growth had been reversed." Interestingly, just like many of the spiritual healers described in this book, Steven did not set out to become a healer. "I had never wanted to do healing. In 1977, I was attending a Spiritualist Church development group. A medium told me that I should be doing healing. Like any 20-year-old, it went in one ear and out the other." However, a few days later, "A friend who was with me hurt his back. As a joke, he said, "You're supposed to be the healer, heal this!" I put my hand on his back and the pain stopped. It stopped being a joke." However, he adds, "One thing I would like to make clear is that I am not a healer. I have no healing powers at all. I am a medium. What I have is the ability to access a power that comes from another source. I can't heal you – but I know people who can! Spirits can bring forth information, or they can bring forward power. A healing medium's job is to access an energy; a healing power… To me and others who practise this healing, God is the ultimate source of the power – but we go through intermediaries. In spiritualist terms, they're known as ministering angels. Usually they were doctors, nurses, people who in life were in the caring professions… when people like that die that desire to help others doesn't just end… and as they no longer have access to medications and other accoutrements of their earthly profession, they are taught a different way of assisting others by becoming spirit healers or spirit doctors."

CHAPTER EIGHTEEN

'Lilley had an unusual use for ectoplasm; sometimes he would use it to grow new living tissue in patients.'

Medium William Henry Lilley was another remarkable medium and spiritual healer. He was born in Yorkshire in 1914 and began his spiritual work at the young age of 15, 'being trained by the spirit world from the age of 10,' according to the National Spiritualists' Union. They say, 'His spirit control, Dr. Letari, could accurately diagnose patients' illnesses and administer healing to them at any distance.' As an adult, Lilley's work took him all over the world, and in one astonishing instance in South Africa, 'Hundreds of witnesses including a number of doctors watched whilst a diseased bone was removed from a boy's upper arm and replaced by a healthy new bone, materialized by the spirit doctor.' Arthur Desmond, in his book about Lilley says that Lilley had an unusual use for ectoplasm; sometimes he would use it to grow new living tissue in patients; or in this case, new bones! Lilley's son David, a homeopath, also wrote about his father's healing

Proof of the Afterlife

work in Healing the Soul. He describes how it all began, when Lilley was taken one day as a young boy to the spiritualist circle his mother belonged to. The location was a walk of several miles on 'a bitter afternoon.' The small group met in a cold room above a village pub and his mother had brought him along because she had no-one to look after him at home that day. They had walked all the way there in the freezing cold; such was his mother's dedication to the pursuit of afterlife communication. As the séance got underway, little William dozed off; or at least, he thought he had, but everyone else saw him rise from his seat and begin to speak aloud in what sounded like a foreign voice, and it was in a pitch far lower than his own child's voice. He spoke with composure and confidence and 'remarkable authority,' ending his speech by announcing that he was the boy's spirit protector, and that William would now go on to do important healing work. William knew none of this until he opened his eyes. From that night onwards, his mother brought him along every week, but on the fourth week, the spirit who had spoken through him was replaced by a new one who announced that he was called 'Ramesoye,' and he told the group that he was an Egyptian doctor 'who had resided in the spirit world for the past 2000 years.' The spirit doctor was speaking through Lilley, and Lilley was now speaking without any sign of his strong Yorkshire accent. The spirit doctor announced that Lilley would go on to become a great healer, and that he and his mother no longer needed to sit in the freezing room above the pub because the little boy's skills would be developed at home instead now. The spirit explained that Lilley no longer required the spiritual energy of the group. Lilley's son describes the relationship between his father and the spirit doctor, who on one occasion was diagnosing one of Lilley's patients and the spirit doctor was in adamant disagreement with the living doctor who had diagnosed the patient. 'Dr Letari insisted that the lung was not the primary seat of the condition and that although the lungs were certainly not healthy, the prime cause lay in the liver with secondary invasion of the chest.' This was relayed back to the patient's doctor. 'The spirit doctor offered the doctor the chance for the patient to receive spiritual healing, to prove what they could do, but the doctor refused to take him up on it. A few weeks later the patient died, and a Post Mortem upheld the spirit doctor's verdict that the cause of the problem was in the liver.' The conclusion of the post mortem was exactly what the spirit doctor had said about the patient's medical condition; in direct contrast with the living doctor, whose diagnosis had been wrong. The ability Lilley now had for communication with the dead, seems to have come from his lineage. Locally, it was well-known that his mother had seemingly supernatural abilities and people would visit her for readings or to receive healing. His grandfather too, although he worked down the mines, was clairvoyant. As for Lilley, he now had the help of the spirit doctor, who according to his son gave his full name as Lejan Tari Singh and said that he was a Hindu from India who had trained in medicine in hospitals in London. He told Lilley he had died in 1914. Lilley could hear the spirit doctor and see him 'just as clearly as we, whose faculties are limited to the earth plane, can see those about us.' Maxine Meilleur writes in Psypioneer Journal in 2013 that Lilley's work became known only through word of mouth initially, until a Spiritualist newspaper called The Greater World wrote an article about him in 1938. This resulted in an influx of requests from the general public for healing and a wealthy businessman called Arthur Richards, who Lilley did not know, also contacted him with an unusual proposition. Arthur Richards was a Leeds based Managing Director of a firm employing 200 staff producing aircraft components, and he had an offer for Lilley: 'Arthur Richards, a metal merchant from Leeds, devised a test for Lilley for diagnosing distant patients merely from an article supplied by them,' a personal item, belonging to the person. Two medical doctors, who had examined the patients, would make their own diagnoses, then seal this up in envelopes not seen or handled by Lilley. Lilley would then make his own diagnoses of the same patients, without meeting or examining them; but by handling a personal item belonging to them. The result of the experiment was that Lilley's diagnosis matched the doctors' diagnosis exactly; in fact, 'Lilley's was far more precise than the doctors.' Lilley said his incredibly accurate insights were given to him by the spirit doctor Letari and Letari's team of medical professionals in the spirit world. The results of the experiment inspired Richards so much that he asked Lilley to train him to be a medical channeler too; but more importantly, Richards financially sponsored Lilley so that Lilley could leave his factory job and devote all of his time to the healing work. Initially Lilley was given a room in Richards' mansion, until a fire broke out. Much of the house was ruined but oddly, the healing room remained completely undamaged by the fire. After this, a sanctuary dedicated for healing was set up in a different premises. Lilley never charged people for healing, and in fact according to Meilleur, he turned down an offer to work at a London hospital, even though they were offering a salary far higher than the sponsorship he received from the generous businessman Richards. The hospital had heard of Lilley's baffling ability for giving precise and accurate medical diagnoses and they wanted his remarkable expertise, even if it did come from spirit. If Lilley had accepted their offer, it's very unlikely they would have made it known publicly. In fact, Lilley found himself hauled into court in South Africa for practising without a license; this came after he had removed the young boy's

Proof of the Afterlife

bone and replaced it with a new one – made from ectoplasm, in front of a large public audience, including medical professionals and doctors. Meilleur corresponded with Lilley's son David, who told her about the spirit operation. He wrote to her saying, 'Desmond Jackson was the young man from whom the humerus was removed. The bone was indeed replaced by ectoplasm and was completely functional. The bone which was removed has been preserved and is still in my possession.' For this 'miracle,' Lilley found himself in court. 'Desmond and his mother appeared in defence of my father and testified in court regarding the remarkable healing… the records of the court proceedings are available.'

William had several healing sanctuaries, including one in Leeds and one in Cheltenham. A reporter for Psychic News said, 'He is a man whose sincerity is apparent, the moment you meet him.' Lilley told the visiting reporter, "It is a tremendous privilege to be used as a terminal for the material expression of the power of the infinite source whose secret has been lost because of materialism over the past centuries." A War-time issue of Psychic News in February 1942 describes how William's application for a license to practice in England was also refused, although he appealed the decision. He was given some help from surprising allies including another spiritual healer called Sidney J. Peters. Peters also happened to be a former member of Parliament and a practising lawyer. To mount

Lilley's appeal, evidence was compiled from 53,000 absent healings carried out by Lilley, in support of their argument that he should be granted a license. The Parliamentarian Sidney Peters had himself become convinced of Lilley's ability to diagnose and heal people after he had tested Lilley. He presented Lilley with the names and addresses of three strangers, along with their ages. This was the only information he gave. In return, Lilley gave "a clear exposition of their maladies for which I could personally vouch." Peters knew exactly what was wrong with these three people but Lilley had never met them; yet he knew too what was wrong with them, thanks to the spirit doctors who told him. In Lilley's biography, Desmond describes other patients Lilley treated, including a lady whose diseased leg would soon have to be amputated, but after contacting Lilley, her leg was completely healed when he gave her distance healing; to the bafflement once more of her doctors. In Sheryl Root's doctoral thesis, The Healing Touch, she says that Lilley had more than just Dr. Letari's assistance from the spirit world. 'He also had many other medical 'helpers', including Dr Cerise in charge of chromotherapy and Dr Moy in charge of pathology, both of whom had been dead for around 250 years, and Dr Turner in charge of obstetrics and gynaecology, who had apparently been practising in London in the late-nineteenth century.' Root quotes from Desmond's biography that when Lilley gave healing to

Proof of the Afterlife

Desmond himself for a range of ailments, Lilley 'performed a 'percussion treatment', tapping his spine to create vibrations: 'Five hundred vibrations a minute, they say, create twenty million vibrations to the spine.' This then affects the medical condition such that 'all the bodily organisms are vibrating, and an organism in disease will be either subnormally lower or abnormally higher than the true vibration.' Lilley said it was therefore necessary, 'to set up in the body a phenomenal vibration which will reproduce a state of energy in any organ sufficient to create a normal physiological action.' This then leads to the correction of the organs so that they can function again normally, he said.

After Lilley died in 1973, Psychic News ran a tribute article about him, and in it they revealed, 'Lord Dawson, physician to three British Kings, once utilized Billy's (Lilley's) mediumship to diagnose a difficult case... Lord Dawson contacted the healer through a group of Leeds doctors with whom Billy cooperated without the fact being publicised. Letari (Lilley's spirit doctor) accurately diagnosed this rare illness.' When Lord Dawson telephoned William to thank him, Dawson asked that thanks also be given to Dr. Letari, who he said, "Had been the means of saving a man's life." The article also mentions another healing Lilley carried out when he was just a lad. 'A boy dying of nephritis (kidney inflammation) had sought out 15-year-old Billy's aid. He was cured in three weeks.' Interestingly, they also describe Lilley's homeopathy, which he combined with his healing work, often prescribing tinctures for his patients. His homeopathy had started rather unusually when Lilley was younger and had taken to going for early morning walks in the countryside after he got home from his night job in the factory. One night, 'An orb of blue light led him to certain herbs.' Taking this as a message, he duly collected up the herbs and took them home with him, where he cleaned them and boiled them and began to give them to many of his patients. After he married, his wife Nancy took over the job of looking after the herb production, while his father helped by dispensing 'the 7,000 stocked remedies.' The article also has more details about the remarkable public operation performed on the arm of the boy in South Africa, because a reporter from the magazine called H. P. Smit was actually there when it happened. Smit wrote, 'Letari conducted a "Psychic operation" unapparelled in the annals of medical science. I witnessed a miracle of healing.' Smit describes what he saw: 'It involved the painless, bloodless removal of a diseased humerous (bone of the upper arm) from Desmond Jackson He was suffering from tubercular osteomyelitis (inflammation of the marrow bone) and could not have been expected by medical science to live long.' Smit was right at the scene; in fact, he was seated just feet away as the operation was performed by spirit doctor Letari, and he had a clear, close-up view. 'Letari said he would ligature the arteries with ectoplasm and divide the arm muscles to permit the diseased bone to be removed.' He continues, 'When the bandages were removed from Desmond's arm, I could clearly see the end of the bone protruding through the skin… Letari, with deft movements so quick that it was impossible for onlookers to follow them, began to remove the diseased bone. Eventually he gently withdrew it from the arm – a sight never to be forgotten… I did not know whether to laugh, cry, or pray, such was my amazement. Some people fainted. Letari held up the bone for all to see... I, as well as others, could clearly see inside the boy's arm!' Then, 'Letari said he would build a new bone. After a few minutes of speedy finger work, he asked Desmond to stand and lift his arm over his head – a movement impossible unless a bone had been replaced in that arm!' Despite this, there was no blood, and no pain, even though the boy had received no anaesthetic. Not only that, but the extracted bone was physically there on view, for all to see. Smit says, 'Before me lay the bone as proof to me and nearly 200 people that what we had seen was not a dream but reality'. After the operation was over, Lilley remarked, "The medical opinion was that entire arm would have to be removed to stop the progress of the disease. Letari used ectoplasm to sever the bone at the elbow, removing and replacing it with a new bone. This meant applying ectoplasmic strands to the muscle fibres to separate them and permit free removal of the bone." As the audience tried to recover from their shock, Smit explains what happened next. 'The Press, with medical specialists, took Desmond to hospital for extensive X-rays.' In the audience there had been a number of medical experts, along with newspaper men, and together they had taken the boy to the hospital to scrutinize what had happened on stage. The radiologist at the hospital said in his report that the new bone was, 'A perfectly normal, regular, healthy humerus.' The new bone, created by the spirit doctor, was a real bone! After the operation, the boy Desmond went on to become a fully active lad, regularly swimming, driving his own car, and boxing! In fact, he lived a perfectly normal life.

Things were not quite as simple for Lilley, who found himself fined in a court in Pretoria for "practising as a medical practitioner." Surprisingly, the Magistrate, P.J. Van der Burg, was actually sympathetic to Lilley's plight, having listened to the many witness testimonies given. He said, "I have reliable people before me who testified that through your skill you were able to cure children classed as hopeless by the medical profession. It hurts me to find you guilty..."

Interestingly, medium trance healer Steven Upton has told me that these days, ectoplasm is no longer used by spirits to heal people. Instead, as fantastical as it may sound, healing is carried out by the following means; spirit healers are able to create 'apports' of body parts. Before this, they carried out transplants, like hospitals do; except the spirits were using the body parts of people who had died! The problem with this was that, just as with hospital transplants, the patient's bodies would often reject the transplant. Or, on-going healing was needed to ensure the body would accept the organ. As a result, spirit doctors have progressed to taking stem cells and DNA strands from the patient to create body parts!

Conclusion

"There are more things in Heaven and Earth, Horatio, than are dreamt of in your philosophy…"

William Shakespeare

I hope you have enjoyed this book. If so, perhaps you would be kind enough to leave a Review. Thank you so much, Steph

Some of these tales can also be heard on my podcast, rated in the top 1% of all podcasts, on iTunes, or wherever you get your podcasts: Unexplained: Tales of Mystery Unexplained

https://podcasts.apple.com/ie/podcast/tales-of-mystery-unexplained/id1216208205

And more episodes here too on

https://www.patreon.com/stephyoungpodcast

Some of my other books include:

Tales of Mystery Unexplained

Tales of Mystery Unexplained Book 2

You can also find me here: Facebook Twitter

Glossary

Cabinet; a small enclosed cabinet which a medium sometimes sits inside in order to make the spirit energy more concentrated.

Closed circle; a private group who meet regularly to develop their clairvoyance and to communicate with the dead.

Development circle/Development group; as above.

Home circle; as above.

Circle; refers to the seating arrangement of a séance, where guests sit usually in a circle around the medium.

Control Spirit; a spirit who takes charge of supervising the other spirits who come through to communicate with clairvoyants and home circles.

Confederate; a person who is physically impersonating a spirit.

Sensitive; old-fashioned term for 'medium'.

Sitters; guests who attends a séance.

Spirit guide; a primary spirit who is with a person all their life.

Spirit Materialisation; when a spirit physical appears.